Introduction and Disclaimer

From the author,

A sincere thank you for purchasing this personal finance book. The information contained in this book is a combination of my 15 years of experience as a registered investment advisor (RIA), mutual fund wholesaler and Series 7 stockbroker.

Unfortunately, personal money management skills are rarely taught in high school or college. Many graduate from high school or college without a basic understanding of personal money managment. This means many individuals may struggle to fully understand the proper use of credit cards, how to manage mortgage debt, how to create a monthly budget and more.

This purpose of this book is to provide easy to digest personal finance strategies that can be implemented in immediately. I wish you the very best in your personal finance journey,

Sincerely,

Andy LaPointe

Disclaimer:

The information in the book is provided for education and informational purposes only. The author and/or publisher is not responsible for the information provided. It is for educational purposes only. It is without any express or implied warranty of any kind, including warranties of accuracy, completeness, or recommendation for any purpose. The information provided here is not intended to be and does not constitute financial advice, investment advice, trading advice or any other advice.

This information is general information and is not a specific recommendation to invest in any investment mentioned or not mentioned. Please do not make may decision to invest, trade or open an account without understanding your own independent due diligence. Please consult a license professional or financial professional. All Information available on or through this book is at your own risk.

Also, feel free to check out the other books in my personal finance series, too.

- Step-By-Step Guide to Investing in Bitcoin: A Beginners Guide to Bitcoin, Digital Assets and CryptoCurrencies
- Bitcoin Smart Kids – Teaching Kids of Every Age About Bitcoin
- Metaverse Smart Kids – Teaching Kids of Every Age About the Metaverse
- Blockchain Smart Kids - Teaching Kids of Every Age How the Blockchain and Bitcoin Work Together

Contents

Introduction and Disclaimer 1

Simple Personal Finance Strategies for a Secure Financial Future 5

Expenses That You Forgot to Include in Your Budget 5

Get Started Right: 7 Personal Finance Tips for the Newly Employed 7

Getting Started in Your Emergency Fund 10

How to Stick to Your Budget While Eating Out 12

Cut Your Grocery Bill in Half with These 4 Strategies 15

7 Habits of Successful Savers 18

11 Tips to Create a Bright Financial Future 21

Do You Struggle with Compulsive Spending? 24

Do You Believe These Personal Finance Myths? 27

14 Way to Save Money During Your Wedding 30

15 Small Moves That Can Lead to Big Savings 33

Don't Let Insurance Fraud Devastate Your Financial Plans 36

A Simple Plan to Regain Financial Fitness 40

7 Signs You're Headed for Financial Disaster 43

7 Steps to Organizing Your Finances 46

7 Ways to Protect Yourself from a Recession 49

Can You Afford to Miss Your Next Paycheck? 52

Does Your Spending Reflect Your Priorities? 54

Habits of Financially Successful Singles 57

How to Eliminate Money Arguments in Your Marriage 59

You'll Be Okay: Financially Adjusting to Divorce 62

How to Raise Cash Quickly 65

Liberate Yourself from Impulse Spending 68

Trying to Build Wealth? Beware of These Strategies 71

Work or Stay Home with the Children? A Financial Perspective 73

Preparing Your Finances for a New Baby 76

7 Critical Actions to Consider Before Trying to Switch Careers 78

Credit Card and Debt Strategies 81

When to Invest, When to Pay Off Debt, and When to Do Both 81

6 Effective Options for Consolidating Your Debt 83

- 8 Good Reasons to Use a Credit Card 86
- A 5-Step Plan for Dealing with Student Loans 89
- All About Store Credit Cards 92
- Anchors Away: Finally Break Free from Credit Card Debt 95
- Get a Handle on Your Debt by Learning How to Deal with Debt Collectors 98
- Signs That You're Carrying Too Much Debt 101
- Top 5 Causes of Excessive Personal Debt 103
- All About Credit Card Delinquency 106
- How Do You Get Out of Delinquency? 108
- 8 Good Reasons to Use a Credit Card 110

Real Estate Strategies 113
- Buying vs. Renting Your Home 113
- Introduction to Budgeting for First Time Mortgagees 116
- Practical Tips for the First-Time Home Buyer 119
- Should You Pay Off Your Mortgage Early? 122
- Why You Might Not Want To Pay Off Your Mortgage 123
- The Top 6 Home Improvements with the Best Return 124
- Tax Tips for Homeowners 127
- What Does Renter's Insurance Cover? 130
- Common Real Estate Investing Mistakes 133
- Beware of These 5 Common Foreclosure Scams 135
- How to Calculate ROI for Real Estate Investments 138

Stress-Free Vacation Strategies 142
- 7 Tips to Save Money on Your Next Vacation 142
- What If... You Had a Vacation with No Bills? 145
- All-Inclusive Vacations Can Save You Money 148

Retirement and Estate Planning Strategies 151
- Renter's Insurance and Retirees 151
- Top Reasons to Revise Your Will 155
- 4 Critical Steps to Retiring When You Want 157
- 7 Effective Strategies to Reduce Estate Taxes 160
- A Quick Guide to Funeral Expenses 162

Basic Investment Strategies 164

Understanding the Time Value of Money 164

Why Do Companies Care About Their Stock Prices? 167

What *Deal or No Deal* Can Teach You About Financial Risk Management 170

Types of Mutual Funds 173

The Tax Advantages of Investing in ETFs 175

7 Ways to Reduce Taxes on Mutual Fund Investments 178

6 Ways to Invest in Gold 181

8 Ways to Invest in Foreign Markets 184

Growth Investing Made Simple 187

Investing in Foreign Stocks 191

Mid-Cap Stocks for Beginners 194

Stock Indexes Around the World 197

What is Bitcoin and Cryptocurrency? 202

How to Avoid These Common Bitcoin Mistakes 204

Deals of the Month 206

January 207

February 209

March 211

April 213

May 214

June 216

July 218

August 220

September 222

October 223

November 224

December 226

Simple Personal Finance Strategies for a Secure Financial Future

Expenses That You Forgot to Include in Your Budget

If you have a household budget, you're doing better than most! **No matter how thorough we attempt to be when constructing a budget, there are usually a few things that escape our minds.** It's the little surprises that can ruin well-laid plans. This is especially true with personal financial matters.

Remember to consider these areas when creating your budget:

1. **Pet-related expenses.** This category includes food, boarding, health care, toys, grooming fees, bedding, and any other supplies you feel your pet needs to be happy and comfortable.

2. **Big ticket items.** *Is there a new car, vacation, or new washing machine in your near future?* These items often slip our minds when making financial plans. Plan for and include these expenses in your budget projections.

3. **Non-monthly bills.** Since most bills are paid monthly, budgets are set up on the same schedule. However, some bills aren't paid twelve times a year. Depending on where you live, the water and trash bills might be quarterly.

   - Automobile registration is an annual bill. This is a small amount in many states, but it can be a very large bill in others. Set aside a little each month if the expense is considerable.

   - Property taxes can be built into your monthly mortgage payment, but this isn't always the case. If you're no longer carrying a mortgage, it certainly isn't the case. Plan ahead.

- Insurance premiums are often paid annually or quarterly. Remember to budget for these.

- Subscriptions and memberships are another non-monthly bill. ***These can include gym memberships, magazine or newspaper subscriptions, and warehouse club membership fees.***

- Home and car maintenance and repair costs can vary from year to year. It's easy to plan for oil changes and furnace filters. But how is your roof looking? What about the tires on your car? These possible expenses can also be budgeted for if you remember them.

- Eye examinations, dental check-ups, and annual trips to the doctor are other expenses that many of us forget when creating a budget. If you need a new pair of orthotics each year, include them, too. ***Consider your regular medical expenses and accommodate for them within your budget.***

4. **Clothing.** Think about your clothing costs over the course of a year and include a line item in your budget. Do you have any special occasions this year? Perhaps a wedding or other formal event will require special financial consideration. Everyone needs to buy clothes on occasion.

5. **Gifts.** Christmas and birthdays have a way of sneaking up on us. It might be a good idea to start saving, and maybe even shopping, in January. Christmas can be a major expense, depending on your traditions and the size of your family.

6. **School-related expenses.** School supplies, field trip fees, school lunches, physicals for sports, and numerous other expenses can add up over the school year.

It's important to account for everything in your budget. ***A household budget isn't very effective if many of your expenses are excluded.***

Get Started Right: 7 Personal Finance Tips for the Newly Employed

Starting your first job is the best time to develop effective personal finance habits - habits that will greatly improve the odds of having a life of abundance and security. ***Good habits and practices are no more challenging to put into place than poor ones.*** So, now is the time to take control of your financial future.

The following habits have been proven to improve the odds of financial success:

1. **Enroll in your company's 401(k) right away.** It's astounding how much money you can save if you get started early. ***If you get enrolled before your first paycheck arrives, you'll never know what you're missing.***

    - It would be difficult to find one middle aged or older person that wouldn't agree with this advice 110%. Aim for a minimum of 10%

2. **Start an emergency fund.** The typical advice is to have enough set aside to pay all your bills for at least 3 months. ***This money will prove invaluable sooner or later,*** whether it's to fix a broken car, pay your bills between jobs, or escape a bad relationship. You'll sleep easier at night, too.

3. **Avoid or pay down debt.** If you're not in debt yet, stay that way. If you are in debt, now is the time to get work on getting rid of it. Debt has a habit of getting worse over time.

    - Develop a plan and stick to it. It will never be easier to get rid of than it is right now.

4. **Stay on top of your credit score.** Some sites, like www.creditkarma.com, provide free scores. You can also get one free report each year from each of the three primary credit-reporting agencies. At the very least, go over your report each year and have the errors removed.

   - ***The primary factors in your credit score are your debt-to-credit ratio and your payment history.*** Avoid using more than 30% of your available credit and pay your bills on time, every time. It's that simple.

5. **Get organized.** There are many things you can do to get organized. Your finances will be much more manageable. Set up a separate email account just for your bills and banking statements. It will be much harder to overlook or misplace anything this way.

   - Set up calendar alerts for your important financial dates. These are things like your rent or mortgage payment and other recurring bills.

6. **Create and follow a budget.** ***Your budget provides a framework for your financial life.*** If you stay within that framework, it's difficult to have financial challenges.

   - A good guideline is to put 50% of your income towards rent, food, transportation, and utilities. Put 20% towards savings and paying down any debt. The remaining 30% can be used for your lifestyle items. These are things like vacations, dining out, and non-essential shopping.

7. **Take advantage of automated savings.** Nearly everyone makes the mistake of trying to save whatever money is left over at the end of the month. There's never anything left over.

    - ***The secret is to never have that money where you can spend it easily.*** Have 10% or more of your pay check sent to a separate account than the money used for paying bills. This can be a savings or brokerage account.

As you can see, none of the suggestions is particularly challenging. Having a great financial life is the result of taking positive action consistently. Get started on the right foot and put these suggestions into play as soon as possible.

Getting Started in Your Emergency Fund

It's always a good time to start an emergency fund. If you've ever needed one and didn't have it, you know just how much it would help to have some extra money available.

The general rule is to have 3-6 months of expenses saved. That's not 3-6 months of salary; it's enough to pay 3-6 months of bills.

Accruing the money will take some time and patience: consider that it would probably take a few months even if you could save every nickel you bring home. But the sense of security you feel when you have money in the bank is the best – even as you build your fund up to a comfortable level.

Here are some simple tips you can use to build up your emergency fund...

- **Cut out Unnecessary Expenses**

    - Do you really need that expensive coffee every day? That coffee costs you around $1,400 a year! Think about where you spend money on a regular basis on things that aren't really that important: eating out, magazines, unnecessary shopping, and more.

- **Save Regularly**

    - If it's just a couple of percent of your take home pay, it adds up.

- **Open a Separate Account**

    - Have a savings account solely for the purpose of holding your emergency fund. That way, you'll know exactly how much you have, and it won't be co-mingled with your other funds. You'll be less likely to spend it at inappropriate times.

- **Have a Sale**

    - Now is the perfect time to empty out the garage, basement, and closets. Sell all that stuff you haven't touched in years. Have a yard sale, put an ad on Facebook Marketplace, or auction items off on eBay. Take the proceeds and put them in that new bank account.

- **Earn Some Extra Money**

    - Consider asking for a raise
    - Find a part-time job or a way to make money online by selling your talents and skills at online freelance sites including:

        - UpWork
        - Designhill
        - LinkedIn ProFinder
        - We Work Remotely
        - Behance

Having an emergency fund is critical to your financial health. Imagine not being able to pay your bills for a couple of months. It can take a long time to dig yourself out of that hole.

Get started today and you'll be in a much better place when that inevitable financial hiccup comes your way.

How to Stick to Your Budget While Eating Out

Eating out is one of life's great pleasures. You get to enjoy a great meal with your loved ones without any cooking or clean up. **When you learn to eat out for less, you can even visit restaurants more often!** Here are some ideas to start saving money today.

Picking the Right Restaurant for Your Budget

1. **Take advantage of restaurant week.** Many communities offer a special restaurant week when some of the most expensive eateries drop their prices to attract new business. They'll probably limit the menu, but you'll get sample creations from great chefs and enjoy the ambiance.

2. **Search for places where kids eat free.** *Look online for places where your kids can eat for free or at big discounts.* Plan ahead for family vacations when you may be eating out for most meals. That way, you'll have a variety of options.

3. **Make the most of your birthday.** You can browse online to get free meals or at least a free dessert or drink for your birthday. Even if the restaurant has no official program, tell them you're celebrating a birthday when you make your reservations and see if they'll throw in something special.

4. **Use coupons.** Sign up for daily deal notices. Pay attention to the details like one coupon per table or a drink minimum.

5. **Negotiate your own discounts.** Many restaurants will offer discounts to nearby businesses to attract repeat customers. *Ask your employer if they've got any deals in place or ask a restaurant owner if they'd consider making some kind of arrangement for customers at a nearby movie theater or gym.*

6. **Enjoy ethnic restaurants.** Ethnic restaurants are often a treasure trove of low prices and great food. Pick your favorite cuisine or tantalize your palate by trying something new.

Ordering Wisely

1. **Spend less on water.** *To avoid surprise charges on your bill, let your server know if you want tap water only.* Even in expensive restaurants, it's up to you whether you want to pay for water.

2. **Evaluate the specials.** Some restaurants promote deals that make the most profits for them. It's okay to ask for clarification on the price even if the server fails to mention it.

3. **Practice portion control.** The servings in many restaurants are far more than one person needs for a single meal. Share a dish or put some aside to take home for lunch the next day.

4. **Approach small plates strategically.** Small plates are a great way to dine. However, you can easily wind up with too much food that will just end up assorted into individual tablespoon-sized dollops of mismatched leftovers. Try ordering a few dishes at a time and ask the server to let you keep the menu. That way you can order more if you really want it.

5. **Consider the mark up on wine.** Wine is another big profit center for restaurants. The mark up can easily be 400% or more compared to retail prices. A great wine can be worth it but consider the investment before you splurge.

   - Meals can be fabulous without wine, too, so remember that you can always elect to save this pricey treat for only the most special occasions.

6. **Go as a group.** Restaurants may be willing to design a limited fixed price menu if you let them know in advance that you're bringing a group. Depending on your guests, be sure to have options for vegetarians and for medical needs such as diabetes and allergies.

7. **Visit at lunchtime.** *You can often get the same dish at lunchtime for around 20% less than the price on the dinner menu.* If the restaurant is slow, they may even be willing to make your favorite dinner dish at lunch, regardless of whether it's on the menu.

Dine well and pay less for the same great experience. If you pick the right restaurants and order wisely, you can have a great time and sample fine cuisine while you stick to your budget.

Cut Your Grocery Bill in Half with These 4 Strategies

It's expensive to feed your family! The cost of food is a large portion of most household budgets, and the price continues to climb.

There are several alarming statistics surrounding the cost of food in America:

- According to The United States Department of Agriculture's Center for Nutrition Policy and Promotion, ***the cost to feed a family of four in July 2022 ranged from $750 to $1,665 a month!***

- Data from the Consumer Price Index shows that food costs have increased an average of 2.8% per year since 1990 and are likely to continue their upward spiral!

Fortunately, there are a few techniques that can help you save big on your next trip to the grocery store!

Use these strategies to dramatically lower your food bill:

1. **Stop paying for convenience.** To realize the biggest savings, avoid pre-packaged foods or foods that have been pre-washed, pre-chopped, or pre-cooked.

    - ***Look for whole foods*** that you can cook and prepare at home, rather than buying food that has been highly processed. Preparing whole foods at home is cheaper and gives you greater control over how much sugar, salt, and fat are added to your meals!

    - Cook at home rather than eat out. If you don't know how to cook, consider asking your friends and family to share their favorite recipes with you. You can also search online for instructions on how to prepare your favorite ingredients.

- Several sites allow users to enter three or four key ingredients and then provide recipes for their use. This is a great way to use up food items that may be close to their expiration date. Therefore, you'll be throwing away less food!

2. **Plan menus around weekly sale items.** Prepare dishes with items that are already marked down or on sale for the week.

   - Many grocers offer specials on items in their meat and produce departments once or twice a month. Other grocers offer significant markdowns on meat, fruits, and vegetables that are close to their expiration date.

   - Shopping early and often can help you identify your grocer's sales and markdown patterns.

   - Most meats and produce can be safely stored in your freezer until you're ready to use them. ***Stock up on these special deals*** and plan your meals around these sales.

3. **Avoid confining yourself to shopping at only one retailer for groceries and other household items.** Look for specials, markdowns, and rewards programs at all the grocery stores in your area.

   - A bigger store chain doesn't necessarily mean better savings! ***Include smaller, regional grocery stores, as well as area farmer's markets, on your list of places to shop for savings.***

4. **Save big with coupons and rewards clubs.** Many stores offer special discounts to members of their loyalty and shopping clubs.

- Sign up and remember to bring your membership card when you shop. Save even more by using coupons you find online.

- Several sites offer coupons for many common grocery items. Many of these sites allow you to download coupons directly to your Smartphone or your favorite retailer's rewards card, so you don't have to spend as much time printing or clipping coupons.

- *Using a coupon on an item that's already on sale will produce extra savings.* Keep in mind that you aren't really saving if you use a coupon on an item that you wouldn't normally buy!

Rising food prices can make it difficult to afford a nutritious diet. These tricks make it easy for you to afford healthy and appealing foods, while dramatically reducing your grocery bill!

7 Habits of Successful Savers

Are you a good saver? Few of us save enough money to maintain a reasonable level of financial security. Many seniors are forced to work well into their golden years. Adopting effective habits can make saving money considerably easier. ***A few small changes might be all you need to have a financially abundant future.***

Saving is a slow process and can require many years to see impressive results. However, your habits dramatically influence your results over time.

Become a successful saver by implementing these habits:

1. **Savers pay themselves first.** Our instincts can steer us in unproductive directions. Many of us feel compelled to pay all of our bills first before saving. It's nice to be out from under the mental burden of bills and other financial obligations. But there's rarely anything left at the end of the month to put into savings.

    - ***Make a habit of saving a percentage of every dollar you earn or receive.*** Start with 2% if that's all you can afford, but make an effort to increase the amount in the future. Avoid spending this money on anything else!

2. **Savers save automatically.** It's much easier and more effective to simply have the money removed from your paycheck before you have the opportunity to spend it.

    - Most employers are willing to split your paycheck and send a portion to a separate account. This might be the easiest way to save.

3. **Savers keep their spending in check.** *The less you spend, the easier it is to save.* Go through your spending over the last month and determine if all your money was well spent. If it wasn't, carefully monitor your spending next month. Think about how much your spending is costing you.

   - It's reasonable to expect an annual return of 10% on your long-term investments. Every $100 spent today would be worth nearly $750 in 20 years if it had been invested. Spending $100 when you were 20 years old cost you nearly $8,850 at 65 years of age.

   - Shop with a list. We've all gone to the store for a couple of small things and come home with far more. Make a list of what you need and stick to it.

4. **Savers avoid debt.** Trying to save while in debt is like walking up a hill and never getting to the top. *Consumer debt is an obstacle to achieving any financial goal.* If you're unable to pay cash, you simply can't afford it.

   - Unless it's for something very important that needs to be paid for immediately in an emergency situation, avoid accumulating any unnecessary debt.

5. **Savers have goals.** *Saving is easier if you have a clear picture of the reason.* The objective of a comfortable retirement or sending your child to an Ivy League school can help maintain your focus.

6. **Savers take regular measurements.** You'll find that most savers are very aware of how much money is in their accounts and how much they've saved and spent. They're on top of their income and expenses.

7. **Savers are financially responsible in general.** They pay their bills on time. They know how much debt they're carrying. They have an emergency fund for the future. Do you know anyone that saves well, and the rest of their finances are a mess? Take responsibility for all aspects of your financial life.

It's possible to save enough money to secure your future and retirement. Having more effective habits will enhance your results. ***With a few minor adjustments, you can watch your savings grow.*** Our lives are the result of our habits. Create habits that support your financial well-being.

11 Tips to Create a Bright Financial Future

Regardless of the type of work you do, it's possible to act now to start creating a bright financial future for you and your family. When you start now, then things like a raise or better-paying job will become the icing on the tasty cake you've already made, and add to your pleasure, rather than having to bail you out of a financial jam.

Try these strategies to ensure your financial outlook is bright:

1. **Save at least 15% of your paycheck.** This amount will give you something to fall back on when times are especially lean or funds to invest so your money can be working for you.

    - For example, if you clear $500 a week, ensure you put back at least $75 dollars for your future.

2. **Find a stockbroker you trust.** As you save your dollars, *it's wise to have an overall investment plan to earn the most interest over the long haul.* However, look at the facts and listen to your gut when it comes to making the final decision on making a particular investment.

3. **Have just one major credit card and use it sparingly.** Charging a small amount on it each month and paying that amount back before the end of the month builds your credit and keeps you out of debt at the same time.

    - *Keep the major part of your credit allowance open for emergencies.*

4. **Vow to never pay finance charges again.** Of course, you'll likely be paying a mortgage and perhaps a car loan that include finance charges you may be unable to avoid. However, outside of those two payments, paying finance charges is like setting fire to your dollar bills. Take steps to insure you pay as few finance fees as possible.

5. **Pay all your bills on time.** There are a few good reasons to do so:

    - You build a positive credit record.
    - You keep money in your pocket instead of wasting it on late fees.
    - You build confidence that you can manage your money responsibly.

6. **Find a competent tax preparer and accept his financial advice.** A great tax accountant will tell you how you can pay fewer taxes and how to rack up some helpful deductions. He may even offer helpful guidance about how much money to put into your Individual Retirement Account (IRA), Roth IRA, or a 401(k).

7. **Set limits with your kids about money.** Teach them from the time they're young that they must earn their own money and save at least 25% of it. ***They'll gain an understanding of money management that will serve them well the rest of their lives.***

8. **Apply $500 to $1,000 yearly extra toward your mortgage principal.** If you prefer, pay an additional mortgage payment each year. It will save you thousands in interest. Plus, you'll pay your home off years earlier, freeing up your funds for whatever you want.

9. **Keep your resume up to date.** You never know when you'll want to apply for a promotion, change careers, or develop side projects for extra streams of income.

10. **Consistently accept part-time, short-term, or temporary second jobs.** ***Bringing in extra money occasionally in addition to your full-time work pads your bottom line.***

11. **Hone your computer skills.** Those who know their way around a computer are more likely to be successful at work. Broaden your horizons even further by learning about new software in your industry.

Put the above strategies to work to strengthen your money situation. Care for your finances and nurture your financial situation today and every day. When you do, you'll live the incredible life you've always wanted!

Do You Struggle with Compulsive Spending?

Compulsive spending involves feeling compelled to spend money on items you don't really want or need. In some cases, you might spend money on items you already have plenty of. For example, even though you love getting new shoes, if you already have 20 pairs of them, it's probably safe to say you don't need another.

Signs You May Be Spending Compulsively

Do any of these signs feel familiar?

1. **You spend all your money as soon as you get it.** On payday, you might pay some bills. Then, any money you have left over, you happily go out to spend. Maybe there's a big clearance on home improvement tools or the dress boutique is having a going out of business sale. Whatever the case, you deplete the monies you obtain.

2. **You use charge cards to buy items when you have no money.** A financially dangerous habit, ***using charge cards to keep buying once the cash is gone can devastate your money and living situations.***

3. **You shop when you feel moody, anxious, or upset in some way.** Your feelings largely depend on whether you're shopping, since shopping comforts you during any stress.

4. **You feel your spending is out of control.** No matter what you do, you just can't stop.

5. **Your shopping causes difficulties in your life.** You perhaps have arguments with your spouse about all the money you spend. Sometimes, you aren't honest about what you spent.

How to Stop

If you experience even one of these points above, there's a real possibility you're dealing with compulsive spending.

Use these strategies to quell your urges to spend:

1. **Make a contract with yourself to stop spending.** Write it out and sign it. Find the confidence to change your direction.

2. **For now, remove credit cards from your wallet.** If you believe you have the fortitude to use a credit card only for emergencies, keep only 1 card in your billfold. Pay cash for everything. Budget your daily cash amount and when you run out of cash, you're done spending (on anything) for the rest of the day.

3. **Contemplate your money situation.** How long has it been going on? How did you get started spending compulsively? Are there specific situations that trigger you to shop now? How do you feel when spending money? ***Work hard to gain an understanding of your drive to spend compulsively.***

4. **Charge yourself for spending.** Every time you spend money for something other than groceries, gas, or utility bills, pay yourself $20.00. This means you must put back the $20.00 to have ready when the bill for the frivolous items comes in.

5. **Write down all expenditures.** ***When you see on paper the amount you spent and what you spent it for, it somehow becomes real.*** In a sense, you're forcing yourself to think about and process what you're doing.

6. **Examine the possessions you already have.** Do you like and use all of them? If you have several debts due to your past credit card spending, think about how you can return or re-sell some of the items you've purchased haphazardly. Then, use that money to pay off the debts.

7. **Recognize spending money doesn't buy you happiness.** Be honest with yourself: has surrounding yourself with stuff you bought with your hard-earned money provided you the life you truly seek?

8. **Empower yourself** by becoming more conscious about how spending affects your life. List the ways your life would change if you had no debt and used money wisely.

9. **Make contact with the Debtors Anonymous group in your area.** Asking for help is the wise thing to do whenever you believe your spending is out of control. Going to Debtors Anonymous won't cost a dime and can provide support for you to get your life back on track.

If you've identified yourself as one who spends compulsively, you've taken a first step in the right direction. Making a contract, avoiding credit cards, charging yourself for spending, keeping track of expenditures, and returning or re-selling unused purchased items will help you get a grip.

Also, listing how your life will change when you stop spending, realizing spending doesn't make you happy, and going to Debtors Anonymous will set you on a positive path to real emotional and financial freedom.

Do You Believe These Personal Finance Myths?

Most adults think they are financially savvy. However, many people hold financial notions that simply aren't true. ***It's difficult to make sound decisions when they're based on false beliefs.*** Adjust your beliefs and you'll strengthen your foundation for sound financial decisions

Beware of these financial myths:

1. **Money and happiness aren't correlated.** Actually, a study done at Princeton University showed there is correlation between income and happiness, to a point. ***Happiness and emotional well-being improve with an increase in salary, up to $75,000.*** Beyond that, however, further increases did not provide additional improvements in attitude.

   - Other research shows that money is a factor in happiness, but it's not the most important factor. The level of respect and social influence a person receives is the most important factor. Of course, money has some influence on these two items.

2. **There is no way that 'I' can become wealthy.** It's not a coincidence that a disproportionate number of extremely successful people come from poor backgrounds. It's staggering how many highly successful people never finished high school. Average people tend to get average results.

   - ***If you struggle to fit into the 'norm', you might be destined for greatness, though it is likely to be challenging.***

3. **There is only one formula for calculating a credit score.** This simply isn't true. The most respected and widely used credit score is the FICO credit score. However, the credit bureaus have their own formulas, and many financial institutions use their own scoring system.

    - All scoring systems result in similar scores about 80% of the time, but there can be significant differences.

4. **There will be enough time later.** Many of us put of saving for retirement or our children's education until a later time. We're under the impression that things will be easier later. *They might be easier, and they might not.* But will there be enough time for your savings plan to be successful?

5. **More education means more money.** In most cases, a higher degree does mean a higher income. Those with a college degree earn approximately a million dollars more over a lifetime than those with a high school education. Those with doctorate degrees average another million on top of that.

    - However, in many fields, those with a degree do *not* earn more. Postal workers and electricians, for example, do not earn more money with a degree. In some fields, those with graduate degrees actually earn less. Editing is an example of one of those fields.

6. **Budgeting is the best way to save money.** A household budget is a great idea, but a budget for a single item turns out to be a bad idea. *People that shop for a single, large-ticket item often spend 50% more if they shop with a budget!*

    - That means, if you're going shopping for a new refrigerator, just go get what you need. If you set a budget, you're likely to come up with the highest number you can afford.

7. **You need to make a certain salary before saving is possible.** Start today. Did you know that the famous TV personality Jim Cramer saved 15% of his income when he was so poor that he lived in a car? How much is he worth today? He is worth nearly $100 million.

Did you believe in any of those myths? Hopefully, you learned something and are now in a better place for making wise decisions. ***Eliminating false beliefs is incredibly powerful.*** Continue learning and your financial expertise will continue to grow.

14 Way to Save Money During Your Wedding

Weddings can be expensive! The average wedding now tops over $27,000. In New York City, the average is over $65,000. The wedding industry brings in over $30 billion!

We all realize that weddings are big events. Anything that involves renting a large space, food, drinks, flowers, and receiving gifts is going to be expensive. But there are many ways to reduce the costs.

Consider these strategies to reduce your wedding budget:

1. **Focus on Fun rather than Perfection**
   Fun is pretty inexpensive. Perfection costs a fortune. Think about a wedding that will be affordable and enjoyable for both you and your guests. Don't worry about everything being perfect. If you worry about making everything perfect, you could end up paying for "perfection" and worrying if everything is perfect rather than truly enjoying that special day.

2. **Be Mindful of the Time of year**
   The summer is the most expensive time of the year for a wedding. Any other time of the year can be 20-30% less expensive. Certain flowers are also cheaper or more expensive at certain times of the year.

3. **Avoid the "Wedding Shops"**
   You can find many of the same items online or at regular department stores. Wedding shops are always more expensive.

4. **Dress Down While Wedding Shopping**

   Some unscrupulous florists may quote a price based upon the car and the clothing of the shopper. Rather the helping you get the most for your money

5. **Skip Engraved Invitations**

   You can save up to $500 by having your invitations thermo-graphed. They'll look just as good.

6. **Consider a Meal other than Dinner**

   Having lunch or brunch at your wedding can save 30% on your reception. You can save even more by having an afternoon wedding with just cake and some hors d'oeuvres.

7. **Check out a Local Park**

   Many cities and towns rent out buildings and parks at a low rate.

8. **Consider Getting your Transportation from a Funeral Home**

   Funeral homes frequently have limousines sitting idle. Consider calling them and get a great deal. Also, this could add more fun to your day. Image sharing the story of riding in a limo from a funeral home to your wedding.

9. **Pass on the Band**

   Hiring a D.J. is much less expensive than a band.

10. **Always Negotiate**

    When it comes to more expensive items, things are rarely set in stone. Aggressively negotiating is the best way to save money on a wedding.

Remember, the vendor can only so "No" if you ask, but you never know until you ask.

11. **Get Everything in Writing**

    If the other party isn't willing to put it in writing, run the other way.

12. **Rent your Dress**

    What happens to wedding dresses after the big day? They sit in a box in the closet until your child tosses it out in 40+ years.

13. **Keep the Photos under Control**

    Photographers can be very expensive. Instead of hiring the same one for the wedding and reception, consider just hiring them for a shorter period of time.

14. **Always Ask Questions**

    Always ask about hidden costs. Ask if the venue charges an extra "venue" tax or adds on a high rate of gratuity. Bring a list of questions and ensure that the vendors are willing to answer every one of them.

Keep these tips in mind when planning your wedding. You can have a super fun wedding without breaking the bank.

15 Small Moves That Can Lead to Big Savings

Most of us would like to establish an emergency fund or pay off student loans. Big goals are great, but they can also be intimidating. **There are small steps that nearly anyone can take to lead to big savings.** Small steps are more comfortable and believable. For example, a moderate diet is easier to follow than a strict one.

Implement these small moves and reap the monetary benefits:

1. **Make one extra mortgage payment each year.** It doesn't have to be one extra payment made at the end of the year, though it could be. Instead, send in an additional 1/12 of a payment each month. *On a 30-year mortgage, you'll shave 5 years off your loan term by doing this.*

2. **Automate your savings.** Maybe you can only save $50 a month, but those regular deposits will eventually grow into a significant amount. Save what you can and do it on autopilot. Pay yourself first and you'll ensure there's some money in the bank.

3. **Watch less television.** Consider cutting down your cable package. After all, how many of those 250 TV channels do you actually watch each week?

4. **Use automatic bill payment.** If you avoid late payments, you'll also avert late fees. Many banks include an automatic bill payment feature with their checking accounts.

5. **Drop your bad habits.** Tobacco and alcohol products are pricey items. *Your health and your bank account will both benefit if you stop drinking and smoking.*

6. **Keep your old car for one more year.** If you can stick it out for one more year, you can delay costly car payments and higher insurance premiums for another year.

7. **Consider refinancing your mortgage.** Do a few calculations and see if refinancing makes sense for you at this time.

8. **Examine your cell phone plan.** You might find that you can go with a cheaper cell plan without noticing the difference.

9. **Shop generic.** *From cereal to pharmaceuticals, there's a lot of savings to be found with generic products.* Some you might dislike, but you'll find many that are exactly the same as far as quality.

10. **Use the library.** Since you pay taxes, those books in the library are partly yours. Go get your free library card and check out a few books instead of buying them. Interlibrary loans ensure that you can get your hands on nearly any book, free of charge.

11. **Buy used books.** Many websites have used books for a fraction of the price. Two such websites are abebooks.com and alibris.com. You can even sell your books when you're done.

12. **Eliminate your home phone.** The number of households with a landline lessens each year. *Since you now have a cell phone, it's hard to justify also needing a home phone.*

13. **Avoid ATM fees.** Stay within your ATM network or get cash back at the store when you use your debit card. It's unnecessary to pay for accessing your money. After all, it belongs to you.

14. **Prevent yourself from overdrawing your bank account.** Some people seem to do this regularly. At most banks, every overdraft costs roughly $35. Even if you're only overdrawn a dollar, you're now $36 in the hole.

15. **Take your lunch to work.** Eating out is expensive, especially if you do it daily. Even fast food costs significantly more than bringing your own lunch.

Are you currently saving money in any of these ways? Could you benefit from adding a few more? Add up how much money you could save by implementing these financial moves and imagine what you could do with all that extra money!

Don't Let Insurance Fraud Devastate Your Financial Plans

You're probably familiar with the concept of insurance fraud, since it has been around for a long time. The earliest recorded instance involves a merchant intentionally sinking his ship in 300 B.C.! The merchant drowned in the process.

You might be surprised at the negative effects insurance fraud can have on your financial future and that of your loved ones. This type of fraud affects policyholders, insurance companies, and investors.

It's not always easy to protect yourself from insurance fraud. This guide explains some of the most common fraud scenarios so you can beware of anything that looks suspicious in your insurance dealings.

While fraud exists in every type of insurance, this discussion is about life insurance.

Insurance fraud exists in two basic forms: buyer fraud and seller fraud.

Buyer Fraud

- **False medical information**
    - This occurs when the insured give false information about pre-existing medical conditions or health habits, like smoking, for example. The applicant is then able to obtain a policy with lower premiums or obtain a policy that might have been denied otherwise.
    - If the insured dies, their family might be denied the proceeds of the policy.

- **Post-dated policy**
  - This is much more difficult to successfully pull-off now and usually requires the knowledge and assistance of an insurance agent. A policy is issued after a person's death but is made to appear to have been issued before that death.

  - Paying fraudulent claims hurts the insurance company and their investors.

- **Lack of insurable interest**
  - This occurs when someone insures another person that they have no business insuring, like if you insured your neighbor, for example. Insurance exists to protect someone from financial loss. If you wouldn't suffer a financial loss from someone's death, you can't insure them to your eventual benefit.

- **Suicide**
  - It's against the law to obtain a life insurance policy with the intention of committing suicide. It's also against the law to commit suicide with the intention of making it look like an accident so an insurance policy can be collected upon.

  - While many policies do pay in the event of suicide, it's only after a specified period of time has passed since the policy was issued.

- **Faking Death**
  - This is largely self-explanatory. The insured fakes his death so the insurance payout can be collected and enjoyed by loved ones or the insured. It's difficult to hide these days, but some still attempt this type of fraud.

Seller Fraud

- **Fake companies**
    - In this type of fraud, a company portrays itself as an insurance company. It issues policies and collects premiums, but never intends to pay on any insurance claims. They simply pocket the premiums and continue doing so for as long as possible.

    - Do your research before purchasing any policy to ensure that the company is legitimate. Check the website of your State Board of Insurance to determine if the company is licensed to do insurance business in your state and the company's status in other areas, like claims complaints.

- **Churning**
    - Churning can be common in any industry where commissions are at stake. An insurance agent encourages his clients to buy a policy, cancel it, and repurchase. The agent can collect greater commissions this way.

- **Premium theft**
    - This is less common with the automated payment systems in use now, but can still occur. The insurance agent pockets the premium and never gives the money to the company underwriting the policy. The agent gets the premiums, and the policy is cancelled for non-payment.

    - To protect yourself from an unsavory agent like this, make your check payable only to the insurance company and check to see who cashes it.

- **Over coverage**
    - Here the agent encourages the client to purchase more insurance than they need. The intention is to collect larger commissions at the client's

expense.

- Insurance fraud has varying effects, depending on the type of fraud:

    - Buyer fraud tends to affect everyone associated with the insurance company, since the costs are spread to everyone. This includes policyholders, investors, and even the company's employees.

    - Seller fraud typically affects individual policyholders and their families or other beneficiaries.

Researching any insurance company or agent you do business with is always in your best interest. Be smart with insurance transactions and you can be confident that your insurance will be there to help protect you and your loved ones.

A Simple Plan to Regain Financial Fitness

Most of us are not financially fit. We are not completely aware of how our money is being spent. We have too much debt and spend money on the wrong things. *While it can be challenging to turn things around, it's well within your reach.*

There is no single, correct path to financial prosperity. Different solutions work for different people.

While there are multiple paths, there are some steps that are critical, regardless of the path followed:

1. **Know where your money is being spent.** Many people only have a vague idea about how much money they make and where it goes. *The first step to financial fitness is know exactly how much you're taking home and where it's being spent.*

   - Websites such as Mint.com make it easy to track how every penny is being spent each month. There are other, similar, services.

2. **Set short-term and long-term goals.** Set a few goals that will cover the next month, year, and five years. How are you going to make these goals come to fruition?

3. **Allocate your spending wisely.** A few simple guidelines will help you to regain your financial fitness. If you're already in a good place financially, these guidelines will help you to stay there:

   - *Keep your fixed expenses to 50% or less of your take-home pay.* This includes things like rent or mortgage payments, utilities, car payments, gas, and food. Basically, the things you must spend money on each month.

- ***Use 20% of your take-home pay to build an emergency fund, pay off your debt, and to save for your retirement.*** It is recommended that your emergency fund be able to cover your fixed expenses for 6-9 months. How the money is split between your retirement, debt, and emergency fund will depend on your situation.

- ***The remaining 30% can be used as you see fit.*** This is the money you can spend on vacations, eating out, or hiring a landscaper. This money can also be put towards the previous category, but be sure to enjoy your life along the way.

4. **Eliminate your debt.** Debt is the most insidious obstacle to your financial fitness.

    - ***Be aware of your credit score.*** There's no need to ever pay to get your credit score. There are many free options available, like CreditKarma.com. Lenders are obsessed with your credit score. You should be even more obsessed.

    - ***Be careful with your credit cards.*** It's always best to be cautious about whipping out the credit card. If you don't have the money in your bank account, it's important to think about how critical this purchase really is.

5. **Get adequate insurance.** What could be worse than finally getting back into good financial shape, only to have it all wiped out by an illness or house fire? ***Protect your assets and limit your liability.***

Reaching a point of financial fitness is a worthy objective. Not only does it give you the opportunity to relax and enjoy your life, it also makes your future much more secure. Allocating your funds properly helps to ensure that you have enough.

Have financial goals and protect your assets. While insurance feels like a painful expense, it really is necessary. A single disaster could be financially ruinous. Get started today and become financially fit.

7 Signs You're Headed for Financial Disaster

Many of us are good at ignoring the negative trends in our lives. Maybe we refuse to acknowledge a growing waistline or a relationship that's slowing deteriorating. ***Many people also ignore the signs of impending financial disaster.*** Most personal financial meltdowns happen over time. They're rarely the result of a one-time event.

The warning signs are quite clear. You simply need to look and be honest with yourself.

Do you recognize any of these warning signs in your finances?

1. **You overdraw your checking account more than once a year.** When you're already struggling to pay your bills with your available income, overdraft fees only make the situation more challenging. Overdrawing your account can be a symptom of these things:

   - **Poor money management.** Some bills simply take longer to clear than others. It's important to do whatever is necessary to stay on top of your pending balance. It can also be a matter of simply failing to pay attention. Having good finances requires regular attention.

   - **Overspending.** Do you have a budget? Are you sticking to it? ***Ask yourself why you are running out of money before you run out of month.***

2. **You're at or near the limit of your credit cards.** Your credit score starts to take a hit when you're above 35% utilization. On a card with a $5,000 limit, that would be anything above $1,750. If you're in this situation, you may be tempted to acquire another line of credit. In most cases, this is only a short-term solution with a poor long-term outcome.

3. **Relying on a future one-time financial event.** Counting on an inheritance or big tax return to balance to your financial situation is a sign of significant debt.

    - *It's important to arrange your finances so that your situation is under control without the need for periodic injections of extra income just to get by.*

4. **A failure to save any money.** A deposit in your savings account can be viewed as just another expense. If you're unable to make that payment, you're headed in the wrong direction financially.

    - All it takes is one unexpected bill or the loss of a job and you're in dire straits. Savings is a better financial cushion than credit.

5. **Borrowing money from family and friends is another sign of impending financial challenges.** Not only is it a sign of financial struggle, it can also be a real strain on your relationships. Most of us loathe asking the people in our lives for money, so recognize the seriousness of the situation if you're considering it.

6. **You're dipping into your retirement funds to pay your bills.** *Stealing from your future is a good sign that the present is shaky.*

    - You're killing the magic of compound interest and likely incurring penalties and taxes by making early withdrawals. You don't have an unlimited amount of time to replace those savings.

7. **Using a home equity loan to fill the financial gaps.** Using a home equity loan to pay bills or to purchase something you can't currently afford is a dire warning sign. Not only are you financially struggling, you're also putting your home at risk. Think long and hard before borrowing from the equity in your house.

If you recognize one or more of these financial warning signs, do yourself a favor and start working on a solution. **When these financial conditions start to pop-up, it's usually only a matter of time before things get significantly worse.** Make strengthening your finances a priority in your life. You'll be glad you did.

7 Steps to Organizing Your Finances

You might not consider yourself to be an organized person, but ***your finances are the last place you want to be disorganized.*** Having too little cash at the end of the month is a challenge, but overdraft fees and late fees every month are an even bigger concern. By getting organized you dramatically cut down on the likelihood of these things happening.

Follow these steps and you'll be more organized that you ever thought you could be:

1. **Look at your budget every month.** Ensure that your budget is accurate. No two months are ever the same, so be sure your budget reflects reality for the upcoming month. For example, electricity bills can be much higher in the summer if you use air conditioning or in the winter if you have the heat turned up.

    - If you don't have a budget, make one now! There are an unlimited number of resources available to make the job a lot easier. ***Budgets are critical.*** Your budget is your key to having your money work for you!

2. **Utilize financial software.** Some of the software available now can really help you to get organized, track your spending and bills, and help with budgeting. Many programs are free.

    - You might actually find working with your money to be enjoyable when you can use a computer and specialized software. It's a whole different experience than laboring over your hand-written figures on paper.

3. **Keep all your bills in one place.** Avoid leaving some of them on the kitchen counter, some in the junk drawer, and some on the desk. Having one specific location for all your bills will ensure that nothing gets lost, and it'll also give you the best chance to ensure that everything gets paid on time.

- Store your bills close to where you normally sit and pay them. Keep them out in the open where you can see them regularly.

- ***When you're done paying them, retain any records you need and shred everything else to protect yourself from identity theft.***

4. **Pay your bills weekly.** Each week, pay any bills that are due in the next couple of weeks. Choose a day and make a habit of paying your bills on that same day each week. Developing good habits is a big part of staying organized.

5. **Make a checklist of your bills.** This should include all your recurring bills. Then, when the bill arrives, you can note the day it arrived, the amount due, the date it's due, and the day you actually paid it. Any non-recurring bills can be added to the checklist when they arrive.

6. **Communicate regularly with anyone who shares your account(s).** Whoever pays the bills needs to know what the other person is doing with the account. Develop a system to ensure that the bill payer is kept in the loop at all times.

   - Financial matters can be a source of stress in relationships, so work out an effective system *before* it becomes a challenge.

7. **Have two accounts.** Mishaps are a lot less likely to happen if you have one account that is only used to pay bills. Use a separate account for everything else.

Getting your finances well organized is a pretty simple task once you set up a system that works for you. ***Anytime you can eliminate financial clutter in your life, your mental chaos goes down and things seem to go more smoothly as well.***

These seven tips will provide a great foundation for your organization effort. Regardless of how you've handled your finances in the past, you can put this plan into action today to make your future financial organizing easy and beneficial.

7 Ways to Protect Yourself from a Recession

Just the word, "recession," is scary for most of us, but you can put many of your fears to rest. By adopting these seven basic principles into your life, the pain of a recession can be largely minimized.

1. **Live within your means.** Living within your means every day is just another way of saying that you should never need any additional consumer debt. ***Once you begin creating debt in your life, more inevitably seems to follow.*** Gas prices may be high, but buy that gas with a credit card at 27% and you'll see just how expensive it can be.

    - Taken to the extreme, if you have a two-income household, you may want to try to learn to live off just one income. Think of the retirement you could fund with the other income. And if one of you should lose your job, you'll already be living on one salary.

2. **Have a second source of income (or a third or a fourth).** A second income source is never a bad idea, even if you just put in a few hours here and there. Job security is practically nonexistent now, and an additional source of cash flow increases your financial security.

3. **Keep a long-term perspective with investments.** Expect that there will be periods of time when your investments will lose money. But you only truly lose money if you sell. The economy almost always improves over time, so you'll make back all your money and then some. In fact, ***a recession can be the perfect time to invest money.***

    - As you get closer to retirement age, move your money into more liquid and lower risk investments. Otherwise, you may not have enough time to recover from any market downturns before you require access to that money.

4. **Consider your risk tolerance.** All the financial gurus have tons of charts and graphs that tell you how much of your money should be invested where, based on your age. But if you aren't sleeping well because your portfolio is down 12%, you may need to adjust your asset allocation. ***You should feel secure in your investments, not be in a state of panic.***

    - Don't sell while the market is significantly down, but when things improve you can move some of your assets into bonds or more stable blue-chip stocks.

5. **Diversify your portfolio.** Keeping your money in different investments will lower your stress and your theoretical losses. You'll also be less likely to do something impulsive. You don't have to get carried away; something as simple as dividing your money between your home, savings account, bonds, and stocks is sufficient.

6. **Maintain a good credit score.** In a recession, qualifying for credit can be challenging enough already. If you want to purchase a house, get a new credit card, buy a new car, or in some places even rent an apartment, you need to maintain your credit scores. Pay your bills on time and keep your credit card balances as low as possible.

7. **Keep an emergency fund.** An emergency fund is an important part of any financial plan. There are many reasons for this. If someone loses a job, there is money available that won't result in an investment loss if used.

    - You never know when the unexpected may happen. What if your car needs a new transmission? Do you really want to be forced to sell some stock that will realize a 25% loss? What if you need money immediately? Some assets can take time to liquidate. And you may need even more time before you can access the funds.

The best part about these suggestions is that they'll serve you well all the time, not just during a recession. Recessions are never easy, but if you make a few small lifestyle changes, you'll ease your burden and reduce financial stress.

Can You Afford to Miss Your Next Paycheck?

Living hand-to-mouth is never enjoyable. But when the economy is struggling, changing jobs isn't easy, and layoffs seem all too possible, living paycheck to paycheck can feel even scarier. What if your next paycheck didn't come as expected? How long could you get by without it? *Luckily, there are some simple things you can do to better your situation and reduce your financial risk.*

Consider implementing these strategies to make your financial situation more secure:

1. **Reduce your expenses.** No one likes to cut back, but reducing expenses is a really fast way to have more money left over at the end of every month.

    - Look at all the things you're spending money on that you don't really need. Do you eat out frequently? Do you have cable television? How many cars do you own?

    - Really take some time and think about what you could do without. Maybe moving to a smaller house or apartment would make sense right now. After all, once you have some emergency money set aside, you can always move back to a bigger place.

2. **Increase your income.** You could do lots of things to earn extra money.

    - Consider asking for a raise. It might seem like a bad time to ask your boss for more money, but ***good employees are always critical to a company's success.*** Don't underestimate your value.

    - A part-time job is another option and, in some situations, this can be a good plan. Maybe you can find some work to do at home in the evenings.

- Even walking the neighbor's dogs, babysitting, mowing lawns or shovelling snow for your elderly neighbors could bring in some extra income on a regular basis.

3. **Take responsibility.** Although your current situation may very well be someone else's fault, blaming others isn't helpful. ***Even if your predicament isn't your fault, solving your financial challenges is still your responsibility.*** After all, who else is going to fix the situation for you?

    - Responsibility isn't about fixating on the past or blaming yourself. Instead, it means taking back control of yourself and your situation. And while you can't have power over every little circumstance that pops up, you can always choose to respond effectively.

4. **Decide that you and your family deserve better.** Circumstances rarely change without a decision being made first. Commit to having to a better financial life, whatever it takes.

    - ***At the end of the day, most people earn what they believe they deserve to earn.*** Almost undoubtedly, there are many people out there with less intelligence and fewer skills than you who are earning more money than you are. Why is this? Primarily because they believe they deserve to earn more.

    - You wouldn't take a job that paid half as much as you're making now, because you believe you deserve to earn more. What if you thought in your heart that you deserved to earn another $25,000 a year? You can be pretty sure that you'd be out there finding a way to get it and you wouldn't stop until you did. It can be a challenge to stop living paycheck to paycheck, but the solutions are relatively simple. Try implementing the practical tips above to ***enjoy greater financial security and experience a less stressful, more fulfilling life.***

Does Your Spending Reflect Your Priorities?

When most of your money goes toward providing what's most important to you, you tend to live a more fulfilled life and feel more satisfied with the way you spend your money. It's also easier to stick to your personal finance plan when its objectives are to get you what you really want out of life.

Because life priorities can differ drastically from person to person, it's important to be aware of your own personal values.

What do you really want from life? What kind of lifestyle do you seek? What are your life goals? Does your spending reflect those things?

Follow these steps to help determine if your finances are in alignment with your priorities:

1. **List your priorities.** You might notice different levels of priorities as you write yours down. Things like having a place to live and plenty of food to eat are your basic priorities.

   - However, you'll most likely include some "necessary" priorities to ensure a strong future for yourself and your family members, like maintaining good health or providing your kids with a good education.

   - Also, list things you love to do that seem more like "luxury" priorities, like reading, traveling or playing golf. These might be on a lower level of priority than your basic priorities, but, nevertheless, they're still important to you, so include these as well.

2. **Now, write down how you spend most of your money.** Where does it go? Although you may get annoyed that much of your money goes toward the mortgage or paying rent, the fact is that we all require a roof over our heads.

    - You might consider the type, size and expense of your home and whether you've gone too far in terms of house expenses. If so, where you live and the mortgage/rent payments might require re-evaluation on your part.

    - Maybe a good portion of your dollars goes to other necessary expenses like groceries and paying your utilities. But what else do you spend your money on?

    - Do you play slot machines on Saturday for fun and end up losing money? Maybe you love to shop and use shopping as a pastime that ends up costing quite a bit. Perhaps you spend $20 a week on coffee and snacks or $30 a week having drinks with your friends.

    - Thoughtfully consider where your money goes from week to week and write it down.

3. **Finally, compare your lists.** Take a look at your first list, the one with your priorities. Ponder each item; does every item accurately reflect what's important to you? Now examine your second list, the one showing where your money goes. Do the lists appear connected? ***Does your money go mostly toward your priorities?***

    - You might be shocked to learn that, even though you listed certain priorities like providing a good education for your children or having a comfortable home, you're spending $100 plus a week on eating out instead of starting an education fund.

- What if you listed reading as one of your priorities, yet you spend nearly $100 a month on cable television you don't watch much? Or if you do, it's the same 3 channels that you'd actually get on a basic cable plan costing less than $40 a month.

- In either case, you've got to ask yourself, "What are my true and real priorities" and "Why aren't I putting my money toward the things that matter most to me?"

Having great clarity in knowing your priorities and being conscious of how you spend your money will help you routinely place money toward what's most important to you. Then, you'll like the way you feel about your finances as funds become available for your favorite things.

Habits of Financially Successful Singles

Some of us enjoy being single and some of us don't. But there's no arguing with the fact that being single can be more financially challenging. *An additional income is a great advantage, and two people have relatively similar living expenses as a single person.* Being single means having to pay for everything yourself.

If you're living life as a single, consider adopting these financial habits:

1. **Limit the size of your home to match your budget.** Only requiring a one-bedroom apartment to satisfy your living space needs is one advantage of being single. It can be tempting to try to compete with your married friends. After all, many of them are likely to have nice homes. Resist this urge and limit your housing to what you really need.

   - Most people spend 90% of their time at home in the bedroom, kitchen, and living room anyway. You can do all of that in a small home or apartment and save your money for more important things.

2. **Successful singles take advantage of being the sole decision maker.** *Being single means having the freedom to make decisions without having to accommodate the desires of others.* It also means there isn't anyone there to keep you honest. Take the time to make good financial decisions. Take advantage of the fact that you're in control.

   - Being married means having to consider the needs and desires of another adult. There is always a compromise.

3. **Travel with a friend.** If you don't have a significant other, traveling can be much more expensive. This is mostly due to paying for accommodations by yourself. In general, a hotel room for two costs the same as a room for a single. Consider going on vacation with a friend or review vacations designed for singles.

    - There are also many options today to minimize lodging costs. Do a search online and you'll be surprised at the many ways to reduce these costs.

4. **Pay yourself first.** This is an excellent habit for anyone, but it's especially important for singles. ***The need for an emergency fund is greater for singles.*** You're the only person paying into it. If a real financial challenge appears, you're the only one available to handle it. Pay yourself first so you're ready for anything.

5. **Take care of business at work.** With a single income, the loss of a job can be especially challenging. If things aren't going well at work, either fix them or start looking for new employment. Many of us do just the minimum at work to avoid being fired.

    - If possible, consider nurturing a part-time second income that accommodates your lifestyle.

6. **Start saving for retirement immediately.** If you stay single, you'll be your only source of retirement savings and investment. You might not plan on staying single, but it's better to be safe than sorry. Besides, saving for retirement is an excellent habit for anyone.

While being single has its challenges, it also has many benefits. You alone control your finances and can make all the decisions. ***The responsibility is on you to make smart choices.*** Minimize your expenses where you can. It's all about saving, protecting your income, and being prepared for the future. Begin adopting the habits of financially successful singles today.

How to Eliminate Money Arguments in Your Marriage

Marital arguments about money have been going on since the invention of money. While all arguments can take their toll, disagreements over finances can be particularly distressing. ***Studies show that money issues are among the leading causes of divorce!*** This is a worthwhile subject to get under control. Not only will your finances improve, but your marriage will strengthen, too.

These steps can keep money arguments to a minimum:

1. **Agree on a budget.** Many couples don't have a budget, but a budget is useful for everyone, even billionaires. ***If you can both agree on a spending plan, many potential arguments can be avoided.*** After all, if someone is outspending the budget, it's difficult to argue about fault.

    - It's practically impossible to get a budget right on the first attempt. ***Good budgets evolve over a few months.*** It will take some tinkering to get it right. Be patient and make the necessary adjustments as you go along.

    - Use the information you already have. Pull out old bills and use some real numbers. Remember to consider expenses that occur less frequently than once a month. New tires, home repairs, and medical expenses are just a few ideas.

2. **Be completely open.** Many couples are exactly sure how much money their spouse is making. Many more spouses are in the dark about their partner's debt and credit history. It's not always easy, but a full financial disclosure can prevent many disagreements.

    - ***Knowing each other's financial status will make it easier to agree on a financial plan.***

    - This includes being honest about all spending. More than a few women hide clothing and shoe purchases from their spouse in the back of the closet. More than a few men buy tools on a regular basis and sneak them into the garage. Be honest.

3. **Set financial goals together.** ***If you're both working toward the same things, it will bring you closer together.*** Partnership and marriage go hand in hand. Sharing a vision is an effective way of limiting arguments.

    - Sit down together and dream big about the future. Then decide how that looks financially. What plans will you have to make? How will you accomplish them? Set a deadline and get busy.

4. **Deal with discrepancies in pay.** In most cases, one spouse has a greater salary than the other. Splitting the bills 50:50 might be fair in one context, but it can also create resentment. One option is to pay the bills relative to the salaries. So, if one person is making $100k, and the other is making $50k, the bills would be split 2/3 and 1/3.

5. **Deal with discrepancies in expenses and debt.** If one spouse has child support payments to make or a large amount of student loan debt, the other might want to consider making adjustments for this when dealing with the bills. Partners help each other out. ***If you want to share in the windfalls, it's only fair to share with the less agreeable things, too.***

6. **Handle disagreements in a healthy manner.** Disagreements will occur, no matter how good the intentions. It's important to keep the discussion centered on behaviors and not people. There's a difference between, *"This purchase wasn't within our budget"* and *"You ruined our budget."*

- When a disagreement occurs, find a solution that will prevent a reoccurrence.

Minimizing money-related arguments is a great way to strengthen a marriage. ***It's also a great way to get your finances under control.*** Many of the steps involved will encourage healthy finances. Protect your marriage and do what's necessary to eliminate money arguments.

You'll Be Okay: Financially Adjusting to Divorce

Are you going through a marital breakup? If so, you might feel like you're in a whirlwind. You're worried. Will you be okay financially? Take a look at the following points to recognize you'll likely make it through, with a few adjustments here and there.

1. **Do the math.** Figure out if you can support yourself financially with the dollars you now earn. ***Remember to include other funds that will be coming in, like child support, alimony, or stock dividends.***

2. **Act now.** If you're going to need a new or different job or additional income, start doing something about it now. If you begin bringing in additional dollars right away, it'll take some of the pressure off later.

3. **Determine monthly expenses.** How much are your monthly outgoing expenditures? Can you count your basic expenditures on one hand: mortgage or rent, car payment, utility bill, food costs, and phone/internet charges?

    - For the other hand, you'll have insurance, entertainment, and savings. ***If you have a lot of monthly payments like 2 or 3 credit cards and more than one car payment, it's time to consider some spending cuts.***

4. **Don't panic.** If you need to make some reductions, decide what you'll cut out. Maybe you can sell one of the cars to eliminate a car payment and reduce your car insurance. Perhaps you'll decrease cell phone charges or cut out paying for your phone land line.

    - Maybe you can combine your 2 or 3 credit card payments all onto one card for 1 monthly payment for everything you owe. If you must, cancel your Netflix account or whatever extra accounts you can do without for now.

- *Once you have your expenses under control and know how your money situation will be, you can add back services you want.*

5. **Take an honest look.** Are you living equal to or below your means financially? Do you and your child really need to live in a 2,700 square foot home? Or could you be perfectly happy in a home that's half the size? Consider this: you'd be paying half the electric bill (you now pay) every month plus lower rent.

    - Once you get some time as a single person under your belt, you can upgrade your standards later.

    - The point is to ensure you're not living right up to the edge of what you make. If you are, it can make for a rather nerve-wracking life. **With some planning, you might be able to reduce your expenses and still live a financially comfortable life.**

6. **Heads up regarding your tax return.** If you're not yet divorced as of the last day of the year (12/31), you can still file jointly if you both agree to do so. Also, if you'll have custody of your children the most, ensure your attorney declares in your divorce decree that you can claim them as dependents.

    - If you're paying alimony, have your attorney include that in your decree. This way, you can claim the amount you pay as a tax deduction.

7. **Take care when splitting up retirement funds.** This issue gets sticky. Talk with your attorney about the best way to handle such funds because, depending on your age and how you do it, you might have to pay early withdrawal fees plus taxes on the withdrawn amount. There are ways to do it without paying these penalties.

When it comes to making it through a divorce financially, recognize millions of people have survived it and you can, too. Recall the toughest times you've had and realize the financial smarts you possess to get through. If you follow the above suggestions, you'll be well on your way to successfully surviving the financial consequences of a divorce. You'll be okay.

How to Raise Cash Quickly

Unexpected financial situations happen to even the most careful among us. When financial emergencies occur in your life, you may find yourself tempted to go for the easiest ways to raise cash. However, there are usually better ways.

If you can keep your wits about you, money can often be raised in ways that have minimal long-term consequences.

Follow these tips to help you calmly assess the situation and determine which option would be best for you.

Be Certain You Really Need Cash

You might not even need cash if your unexpected expense is relatively small. Maybe you have some gift cards to stores or restaurants that you've forgotten all about. Also, some credit cards have reward programs that frequently go unused. Some of these pay cash and others build points than can be redeemed for merchandise, gift cards, and more.

Quick Money Schemes to Avoid, if Possible

1. **Family loans.** Borrowing money from family and friends can be a positive or negative experience. Whether or not this is a good option for you really depends on your unique situation.

    - Consider the likely outcome if you are unable to pay them back as agreed. In many instances, if such likelihood occurs, it can cause hard feelings for a long time.

2. **Payday loans.** *Some of the worst ways to raise cash are loans that come with very high interest and fees.* Payday loans are an easy way to raise money quickly, assuming you're employed. But when you consider the interest and fees associated with these loans, you could easily end up paying them back twice as much as they lent you – or even more!

3. **Title loans.** Loans that use your car title as collateral are not only very expensive, but they are also quite risky. *If you can't pay as agreed, you'll lose your vehicle.*

4. **Cash advances from credit cards.** These advances are another expensive way to get your hands on some cash. While credit card purchases don't usually start accruing interest immediately, cash advances do.

Better Options

While still not your best option, you can withdraw money from your retirement account. *Here's a loophole you can use to avoid taxes and penalties:*

If you transfer your IRA into a new IRA account, you have the option of having the money sent directly to you, on the condition that you deposit the money into a new IRA account within 60 days. If you can replace the money in that time frame, you're getting an interest-free, penalty-free, and tax-free loan. You can only do this once each year.

If an IRA transfer isn't an option for you, you can also sell savings bonds that haven't yet matured. Also consider selling your stamp, coin, or jewelry collection. Keep in mind that if you're going to sell them quickly, you're unlikely to get a good price.

Your Best Choices

1. **Sell some liquid investments.** *Selling items from your non-retirement portfolio is, for many people, the best way to raise some money.* First, sell those items that have been stagnant and show no signs of doing anything in the near future.

2. **Borrow from your 401k.** However, there are penalties and taxes if you fail to pay the money back.

3. **Take out a home equity loan.** A home equity loan is a viable option for some; just keep in mind that you are putting your house at risk if you can't pay back the loan.

Planning Ahead

Having an emergency fund is critical to negating the effects of financial emergencies. Strive to save 3-6 months of expenses and leave the account alone unless you have an actual emergency. This is the most fundamental step you can take to ensure your financial security.

Avoid letting a challenging situation become even worse by making a hasty decision. First, decide if you really need cash. Maybe a non-cash alternative is available. If this doesn't work for your situation, do some planning before you decide how to proceed. Be sure to thoroughly investigate the fees and interest rates that are associated with your options.

Although unexpected expenses can bring with them tension and high emotions, remember that making a good choice now will result in fewer headaches later. Take as much time as you can to make the best decision for you.

Liberate Yourself from Impulse Spending

Wherever you go, retailers are trying to get you to buy more and spend more. If you want to stick to your budget and avoid purchases that you later regret, there is hope. Try these simple steps before, during and after your next shopping spree.

Steps To Take Before and After Shopping

1. **Shop on a full stomach.** Eating first has always been an effective way to spend less on groceries and it works on other items too. *You think more clearly and feel less pressured when you're well nourished.*

2. **Make a list.** Etch your purpose firmly into your mind. You may still decide to pick up unexpected bargains, but you'll be less likely to wander around gathering random stuff.

3. **Reduce your exposure to advertising.** Hit the unsubscribe button on those junk emails. Throw catalogs directly into the recycling bin. Go do some leg lifts while TV commercials are playing.

4. **Conduct an inventory.** Take a good look at what you already own. Maybe there's an old desk in your attic you can spruce up with some paint rather than buying a new one. Pondering ill-advised purchases will also reinforce your determination not to add to them.

5. **Research prices.** Learn what constitutes a good value. That way you'll be less vulnerable to extravagant claims. A jacket that's marked 80 percent off may have started out with an inflated price.

6. **Exercise your mind and body.** A Washington State University Study found that *students who performed regular mental or physical exercise for as little as two weeks were less tempted to engage in impulse buying.* Take a daily walk or read more books.

7. **Focus on nonmaterial rewards.** Seek gratification from helping others, spending time with loved ones and improving your mind. It will make the mall look less interesting.

Steps To Take While Shopping

1. **Limit your browsing.** At the mall or online, make your purchases and leave. *The longer you linger, the more items you'll be tempted to buy.*

2. **Shield your eyes at the cash register.** Grocery store tactics are spreading. Checkout lines everywhere are now surrounded with candy and other last minute temptations. Distract yourself by checking your phone messages or planning what to make for dinner.

3. **Pay in cash.** *Studies show that customers who use cash spend less than those who use credit cards.* Cash makes you more aware of how much money you're forking over.

4. **Give yourself time to cool off.** *Slow down and give yourself time to think before deciding to complete a purchase.* The bigger the price tag, the more time you may want to devote getting it right.

5. **Be skeptical about limited offers.** Some marketing campaigns try to make sales by talking about limited time offers and scarce quantities. Vermeer's are rare. Nail polish and sneakers are not.

6. **Remind yourself of the disadvantages to any purchase.** It's easy to get caught up in how much you want that shiny new gadget, so keep the whole picture in mind. Most products are very temporary and you may have more important uses for the money.

7. **Take along a friend.** Shopping with family and friends may provide you with more objective feedback than you'll get from a salesperson working on commission. A second opinion comes in handy when you're trying to make a sound decision.

Protect your financial well-being and get more pleasure out of your possessions by becoming a smart shopper. With a little thought and practice, you'll learn to manage your impulses and feel good about your purchases even after you get them home.

Trying to Build Wealth? Beware of These Strategies

Who doesn't want more money? Even people with billions of dollars seem preoccupied with trying to get even richer. But why do some people seem to acquire money easily while others really struggle?

I'm sure you've noticed that many financially successful people aren't particularly talented. The difference is that they're spending their time on productive and profitable things.

At the end of the day, people are paid in relation the amount of value they provide. To receive money, you simply must be creating value in some way.

There are many ways to provide value; just think of all the things in your life that you're willing to purchase. This isn't a complex idea, either. For thousands of years, people have been trading value for income. If you haven't fully internalized this concept, you might be spinning your wheels in trying to build wealth.

Consider these two habits that may be coming between you and real wealth:

1. **Using mental gymnastics as a means to generate income.** The idea of generating wealth via meditation or visualization has become very popular. Books like *The Secret* and numerous similar programs have suggested that merely focusing on what you want will seemingly cause it to drop from the sky into your lap.
    - Admittedly, ***these practices can be very helpful*** because working on your mental blocks is always a worthwhile endeavor. But these activities *in themselves* do not directly generate income. Do these practices provide any value to anyone else?

- Your mental housecleaning may very well put you in a better position to create value for others, but the housecleaning itself doesn't matter to other people. And no value equals no money.

- Making a lot of money usually takes a lot of action. ***At some point, you need to stop the mental cleansing and begin taking physical action to create the value that precedes getting paid.***

2. **Focusing on the money instead of value creation.** In some ways, this is related to item #1. Always ask yourself if you would be willing to pay for the "value" that you've created.

    - Websites are an excellent example. There are several great websites out there that provide tremendous value, and people are willing to trade their money for that. But there are countless sites that are not of much worth. They offer the same articles, posts, and perspective that can be found on 100 other websites.

    - ***Those poorly executed websites were created with the idea of generating income, not providing value.*** In these cases, the website is being used as a tool in an attempt to milk a system, rather than as a tool to provide value. In your quest for money, avoid selfishness. You have to give before you can get, just like you learned in kindergarten.

Trying to "meditate" your way to a million dollars makes for great marketing, but doesn't directly provide income. ***Real action also must occur.***

Focusing only on the money without a thought towards providing value doesn't make a good business model. ***Work on creating value and then charge people for it.*** You'll be wealthy before you know it.

Work or Stay Home with the Children? A Financial Perspective

Deciding whether one or both parents should work is never easy. There's not a single approach that will work well for all families.

There are many potential cost savings that can be gained by a parent staying home to care for the children. On the other hand, there is also a loss of income.

Analyzing the details for your own situation is your best bet.

Sometimes couples have more options when one spouse has a significantly higher paying job or more work flexibility than the other. Many people believe that nearly any couple can afford to live on a single income, because childcare and other expenses linked to work usually use all of the second income. But this isn't always the case.

Let's take a look at some numbers associated with one spouse staying home:

- **Child care savings.** $600 to over $1,000 per month for childcare is not an insignificant amount.

- **Wardrobe savings.** Most of us need clothes for work that cannot be satisfied by the clothes we typically wear at home. Remember dry cleaning costs as well.

- **Commuting savings.** You might only need one car instead of two. Even if you keep two cars, the cost associated with gasoline, tires, maintenance, and more will be greatly reduced.

- **Food savings.** If you stop going out to eat, you can save a bundle. If a spouse stays home, that can cut down on lunch costs and expensive coffees.

- **Home-based income.** Maybe one parent can telecommute part-time. ***There is also the opportunity to start a home-based business that could result in significant income.*** This item might require part-time day care, nursery school, or simply waiting until the child is old enough to start regular school.

- **Frugality.** If you use this opportunity to overhaul your entire way of life, you might save a bunch more through simple living. A lifestyle that highlights frugality can be a wonderfully simple and meaningful way to live.

When It Might Make Sense to Keep on Working

1. **You're already frugal.** If you're already a penny pincher, your main savings when moving to a single income will be childcare.

2. **Mortgage qualification.** A second income can make it easier to qualify for a mortgage. But be careful, if you can't qualify with the one income, you might be on thin ice if you ever decide – whether by choice or necessity – to live only on one income.

3. **Retirement Income.** You can miss out on a lot of retirement savings and 401(k) contributions by staying home.

4. **Future ability to be employed.** Is your current career important to each of you? ***Dropping out of the workforce can stop your career cold.*** Consider where you would be likely to be in 10 years if you continued working. You might not even be able to start at the same level you left.

5. **Divorce.** The divorce rate means it's more than likely that you'll be a single parent at some point. Having your own household is obviously more expensive than living with someone else. Sadly, most couples don't grow old together. So consider the ramifications a divorce would have on the financial situations of everyone involved.

One parent staying home with the children can be wonderful for the kids. It can also be a financially reasonable solution, depending on the specifics.

Consider the long-term impact and decide if it's the right move for your family's situation.

Preparing Your Finances for a New Baby

A new baby on the way is always an exciting and celebratory time. However, a baby can also be a huge financial challenge, especially if you don't take the appropriate steps to prepare yourself. Keep these tips in mind when preparing your finances for the new arrival.

New Baby Expenses

1. **Medical bills.** *Find out in advance what medical bills you're likely to incur.* This would include prenatal, delivery, and postnatal expenses. Do you have insurance? How much will it pay? If you don't have insurance and have low income, your state has programs that will minimize the expense.

    - Plan ahead. Depending on your insurance situation, you may want to have additional funds set aside for unforeseen medical issues.

2. **Baby items.** Here we're talking about things like car seats, strollers, changing tables, cribs, bottles, clothes, diapers (2,700 just the first year!), rocking chair, swing, dresser, baby monitor, and more. Go out to your local store and price these items.

    - Are you going to breast-feed? You may need a breast pump if you plan on ever leaving the house without the baby. If you're not breastfeeding, you'll need bottles, nipples, and formula.

    - Do you need day-care or a baby-sitter? Call around to compare costs or ask a neighbor or friend what the going rate is for daycare in your area.

Lower Your Costs

1. **Borrow and buy used.** *Babies outgrow things long before they wear them out.* You shouldn't have any problem finding quality used baby clothes, toys, and furniture. There are even stores that specialize in used baby items. You can also check on Craig's List.

   - These used items can be much less expensive than new stuff.

   - When the time is right, tell everyone you know about your happy news. You'll almost certainly be offered plenty of baby-related items.

2. **Wait for gifts.** People can go crazy giving gifts when a baby is involved. You never know what you're going to get. Wait until the dust settles before you start making purchases. The gifts you receive can be a real financial boon. Be patient so you don't get stuck with two of the same thing.

3. **Remember that you don't need everything.** Your baby doesn't require every gadget under the sun to be safe and happy. Ask the mothers you know what they consider to be the most important items.

4. **Start saving now.** *You can never start saving too soon.* Now is the time to eliminate all those things and services that you don't really need. Sit down and look at your monthly bills and find ways you can cut back. Reduce your expenses as much as you need to so you can save enough money to be as comfortable as possible when the baby arrives.

5. **Review your life insurance and will.** Sit down with the appropriate expert to ensure you have the proper insurance coverage when the baby arrives. Also be certain that your will is up to date. Preparing for a new baby can be an exciting time. For the smoothest first year for you and your little one, remember to include financial preparations as well.

7 Critical Actions to Consider Before Trying to Switch Careers

Most people change careers several times over the course of a lifetime. Perhaps the career we chose in our younger years turned out to less than satisfying. Or maybe our field has been displaced by technology. Sometimes we simply want to try something new and exciting.

Changing careers is common, but there are potential pitfalls. *A little planning can make a big difference in the smoothness of the transition between careers.* Planning ahead is a good idea because you're much more likely to end up with a career that you can love for years to come.

Consider these items carefully before making a career change:

1. **Think about the financial implications of the change.** If you've progressed well in your current field, it's unlikely that you'll soon be able to replicate that salary in your new field.

    - Do you have the necessary financial resources to make the career change now? Assume the transition will take some time.

2. **Start working on your resume and interviewing skills.** *If you haven't looked for a job in the last 20 years, your resume and job hunting skills could probably use an update.* You'll find a much better job if you polish those skills before starting your job search. There are countless books and consultants available to help you brush up.

3. **Run to something, rather than away from something.** When people are miserable, they tend to gravitate towards anything that looks better. However, there are more beneficial ways to make the decision.

    - Any exit looks good when the building is on fire. You're much more likely to be happy with your career change if you take the time to choose the best field for *you*.

    - The more you dislike your current job, the more important it is to take a deep breath and examine all of your options.

4. **Avoid a career decision based on financial considerations.** Of course, salary is a part of the decision-making process, but using it as the sole criteria can yield disappointing results. ***Money, even a large amount, probably won't make up for spending 8+ hours a day in misery at your job.***

    - People that are stressed tend to have more health issues, which are expensive, too.

5. **Decide if you need a new career or if you just want a new job.** Some people are miserable in their jobs, but that doesn't necessarily mean a new career is required. Maybe the solution is as simple as taking a similar job at another company. Perhaps the issue is just your boss.

6. **Find a new job before leaving your current position.** Predicting the amount of time it will take to find a new job is like trying to predict the lottery numbers. It might take a week. It might take 12 months or more.

    - ***Unless you have significant financial resources, secure your new job before quitting the old one.***

7. **Obtain the necessary training and education first.** Many people try to change careers before having the necessary credentials in place. You might have to volunteer or be a temporary employee to get the necessary experience.

    - Do you need any certifications or a license for your new career? Do you need to go back to school? Your current employer might pay for your classes.

Life is short, and changing careers is one way to pack more fulfillment into your years. It's also common to grow disenchanted with a career after doing it for too long. ***Switching careers is exciting, but it also requires some thought and planning.*** Take the time to find the best career for you and ease the challenges of the transition.

Credit Card and Debt Strategies

When to Invest, When to Pay Off Debt, and When to Do Both

If you're facing the dilemma of paying off debt or investing your money, you might also be wondering if you can come out ahead with some combination of both.

Fortunately, there is a middle ground that allows you to pay off your debt while making smart investments to increase your current income.

Sometimes, investing instead of paying off debt may even be a more cost-effective decision. If your investment yields earnings greater than the interest on your debt, your money is better spent on those higher yield investments.

Let's look at different scenarios to help you determine the most lucrative options for your own situation:

1. **When investing is a better option.** You may have a mortgage or student loan debt that carries with it a set monthly interest rate. ***Whether or not the interest from these loans is tax deductible may influence your decision to invest or pay off the debt.***

    - If the debt costs you less money per month than you could otherwise earn through profitable investments, then it is in your best interest to focus on investing.

2. **Say "yes" to free money.** If you currently have debt and are employed by a company that offers a 401k plan, you are turning away free money by not enrolling. Saying "no" to a 401k is essentially leaving money on the table.

3. **When it's better to pay off your debt.** Of the many different kinds of debt, ***credit card debt often carries with it some of the highest interest rates in the industry.*** These interest rates can now be as high as 18% to 23%, and trying to find investment options that yield such a percentage in earnings may prove difficult.

    - Until you find an investment option that provides you with that percentage amount in returns, it may be in your best interest to focus exclusively on paying off the debt.

4. **Investing and paying off your debt.** You may now be seeing the bigger picture regarding debt and investing. In essence, it is a balance of interest rates.

    - ***Finding a balance where you are paying off your high-interest debt while investing in stocks that also provide a high percentage in returns is ideal.*** The investments will be more cost-effective than paying off your low-interest debt.

If debt is like a leaking boat, the best step is always to plug the largest leak first. High interest credit card debt is by far the largest leak and should be considered a top priority.

It's also important to consider the fact that many loans can be paid in advance. Paying a loan in advance is always the best return on your capital and should be done whenever possible.

If you're still deciding on whether to pay off your debt or invest, ***make a list with your debt on one side, and investment options on the other side.*** Compare the interest rates from both sides and decide which require your attention first. Then your plan will be your most lucrative solution.

6 Effective Options for Consolidating Your Debt

Many consumers have a variety of debt. All the payments and different due dates are enough to drive anyone crazy. ***Wouldn't it be nice to address all of your consumer debt with one, simple, monthly payment?*** There are many options for consolidating your debt into a single loan and eliminating some of the stress from your life.

Examine these debt consolidation options that may be available to you:

1. **Credit card consolidation.** You've seen the offers for 0% interest on balance transfers and purchases for the next year or two. These can be an effective way to transfer all of your debt to a single card and avoid interest payments for a while.

    - For balances that are unable to be transferred, the credit card could be used to pay off the debt.

    - Read the small print. Even a single late payment can cause the interest to kick in. In most cases, the interest is actually accumulating from day one. You only have to pay it if you miss a payment. One missed payment can send your whole plan down the tubes.

    - ***It's important to be diligent and ensure all payments are made on time every month.***

2. **Life insurance loan.** If you have a life insurance policy with cash value, you may be able to borrow against the value of the policy. The loan doesn't even have to be paid back. But it will reduce the amount your beneficiaries receive.

3. **Personal loans.** If you have a friend or family member with the financial means to help, you might be able to get a personal loan. If your credit is poor, this might be the only option available to you. However, realize that your relationship could be at risk.

    - A legal document spelling out the terms of the loan can put the lender's mind at ease.

4. **Student loans.** Your credit card limit might not accommodate a student loan, but there's an entire market for student loan consolidation. Since the government guarantees the loan, these loans are easy to get.

    - ***You can consolidate multiple student loans into a single loan and payment.*** It's even possible to have the payback period extended.

5. **Home equity loans.** If you secured a great deal on your home or have been making payments for a few years, you have equity in your home that can be used to pay off your other debts. The interest rates are usually quite low because your home is serving as collateral.

    - Home equity loans can be a convenient and reasonable way to pay off higher-interest debt. However, ***you're also putting your home at risk should you get behind on your payments.***

    - It's also possible to refinance your home and get cash at closing. There are closing costs to consider, but it's very similar to having a home equity loan. Refinancing will permit you to pay back that cash over the lifetime of the mortgage.

6. **Retirement plan loans.** Many retirement plans permit the account owner to borrow funds for specific periods of time. You'll be charged a small amount of interest. The interest payments go into your account, too!

- There isn't a credit check, but you'll be charged an early withdrawal penalty and taxes on any funds you fail to pay back.

If you have too many debts to manage, debt consolidation might be a good option for you. ***Debt consolidation is an effective way to deal with high-interest debt by lowering or eliminating the interest altogether.*** Debt consolidation is another tool to keep available in your financial tool belt.

8 Good Reasons to Use a Credit Card

Personal finance gurus spend a lot of energy attempting to prevent us from using credit cards, usually with good reason.

Credit cards are frequently abused and are the cause of a lot of personal debt. *However, credit cards bring you a lot of advantages as long as you use them wisely.* In fact, credit cards are frequently a better way to pay for things.

Consider these benefits:

1. **Signup bonuses.** Many credit cards offer significant rewards when used responsibly. For example, consumers with good credit can be approved for credit cards that offer signup bonuses. These bonuses can be worth $50 to $250 or even more. Some credit cards provide points that can be used to redeem rewards like gift cards or airline tickets.

2. **Cash back.** With the right credit card, you can earn from 1-5% back on all your purchases. *Depending on how much you use it, that can be like getting a raise at work.*

3. **Investment rewards.** Some credit cards, such as the Fidelity Investment Rewards card, give a higher rate of cash back. However, that cash back must be deposited directly into an investment account. This is also nice because it encourages you to invest and save.

4. **Frequent-Flyer miles.** Nearly every airline has at least one credit card offering. The ultimate value of these cards is really determined by the specifics of the card and the airline tickets you actually receive and use. The details can vary so shop around.

5. **Safety.** Using a credit card makes it a lot easier to avoid financial losses due to fraud or unfortunate timing on automatic payments.

    - For example, if you pay your bills with automatic payments directly out of your checking account, these automatic drafts can also potentially result in insufficient funding fees and late payments, which will have a negative effect on your credit score.

    - If your debit card is used fraudulently, your money is taken out of your account instantly. It can also take some time to get your money back. By comparison, **when your credit card is used fraudulently, you don't lose any money;** you simply notify your credit card company and you don't have to pay for those transactions.

6. **Grace period.** Credit card usage gives you time to pay, usually a couple of weeks on the average before any interest kicks in. With a debit card, the money is gone instantly. If you have your money in a high-interest checking account, the amount of interest you will earn can be significantly more over time by paying for your purchases with a credit card.

    - When you put your purchases on your credit card, your money will spend more time in your checking account, where it's earning money for you. If you use a debit card for your purchases, the money is in your account for a much shorter length of time, thus earning less interest.

7. **Insurance.** Most credit cards include a plethora of consumer protections that most people aren't aware of. This includes things like rental car insurance and travel insurance. Some product warranties are also made more advantageous when you pay for the item with your credit card.

8. **Building credit.** If you don't have a credit history or if you need to improve your score, a credit card can help raise your credit score. Obviously, this assumes that you use your card wisely. Debit cards do nothing to help your credit score.

See, credit cards aren't all bad! ***Provided you can use them responsibly, credit cards potentially have a lot to offer.*** So dust off that credit card and put it to good use; just be sure to pay it off in full every month.

A 5-Step Plan for Dealing with Student Loans

The nation's student loan debt is over $1 trillion and is not only larger than the country's collective credit card debt, but there are also 5 million ex-students that are delinquent with their payments.

Student loans are unique in that they're one of the few debts not discharged with bankruptcy. **Only a federal judge can let you out of your obligation to pay and they don't do that often.** The only reliable way to get out of your student loans is to pay them off.

People frequently get into trouble with their student loans, and it makes getting mortgage or a car loan much more difficult. While credit repair agencies can do a lot to help remove bad credit history attached to debts that are paid off, current debts are another story. A slip can haunt you for a long time.

This process makes it easier to handle your student loans effectively:

1. **Assess your situation.** Student loans can be confusing. You're likely to have more than one loan and those loans were probably made by different financial organizations. The company servicing the loan might be completely different from the one that provided the loan.

    - A great central source of information is the National Student Loan Data System www.nslds.ed.gov. *This resource may provide all the important dates and other information about your loans, including the services.*

    - However, private student loans are not covered in that data system. Your credit report can provide information. Also, contract the college, too.

2. **Ensure your information is current.** For example, the address listed probably belongs to your parents. When you have your own address, you should change your information accordingly.

    - Update all the applicable information, including your email address and phone number. You want to know when there is an issue with your account.

3. **Create a strategy for repayment.** *Your options depend on whether your loans are federal or private.*

    - Federal loans have very flexible repayment options. You can extend your payments out as far as 25 years. You can establish a plan with lower payments now and higher payments later on. Payments can even be a function of your income.

    - There can be other options for private loans, but they will vary, depending on who made the loan. Be sure to give them a call and see what other options are available.

4. **Consider automatic payments.** Federal loan interest rates are reduced by 0.25% if you have your payments taken automatically out of your bank account. Similar deals are usually available with private loans. Either way, you'll never be late if the payments are taken out of your account automatically.

5. **Be focused.** *It would be wiser to put any extra funds towards higher interest rate debt.* But if your student loans are your only real debt, then put some extra money toward the principal when possible. Debt is like a slow leak that keeps draining money away from you.

- Consider a second job to get rid of those loans quicker. The interest rates are relatively low on student loans, but the payback period is long.

- Create a goal of making all of your payments on time. Create a second goal of paying your loan back early.

Dealing with student debt is a big responsibility. It might even be a newly graduated student's first big responsibility. **While making loan payments is never fun, it's a fact of life for most adults at one time or another.** Get on top of the situation now, and the future will be much brighter.

All About Store Credit Cards

Many of us have and use store credit cards. ***We're commonly enticed to complete store credit applications by promises of discounts and rebates.*** But are these store credit cards a smart decision? It isn't easy to know. A little self-evaluation is likely to yield the best answer.

Stores issue credit cards in hopes that you'll shop in their stores more frequently. They're also betting that you won't pay your full balance each month. Companies that issue credit cards make a lot of money from interest payments and late fees. Be cautious and avoid falling into those common traps.

Store credit cards can be useful, if they're used correctly. The savings can be great, but the interest rates are high. ***The value of store credit cards is largely dependent on using them responsibly and intelligently.***

As with anything, there are advantages and disadvantages to using these cards:

1. **Credit.** An additional line of credit can be useful. It's another opportunity to build your credit history and boost your credit score. It's important to use credit wisely. Another line of credit is also another opportunity to create additional debt and financial headaches.

    - ***The greater your total credit limit, the greater the potential for financial disaster.***

2. **Discounts.** Holders of store credit cards frequently receive discount offers. It's also common to receive coupons in the mail. The savings can accumulate over time and add up to a considerable amount.

   - ***It's important to take advantage of discounts and coupons offered through store credit cards rather than essentially giving them back by carrying a balance on your account.***

3. **Rewards.** Many store credit cards also have perks. These might be in the form of rewards points that can be redeemed in some fashion. Similar to traditional credit cards, free merchandise or gift cards are the norm. It's also possible to receive other perks, like free gift wrapping.

4. **Interest charges.** Of course, if you pay your balance in-full each month, the interest is irrelevant. Credit card companies know that most consumers will eventually carry a balance and return those discounts back in the form of interest payments.

   - Store credit cards have some of the highest interest rates out there.

5. **Limited use.** ***Using store credit cards is limiting because you can only use them in the store that issued the card.***

Store credit cards can potentially be a valuable financial tool because there are significant savings to be had. However, be responsible with these cards. ***Store cards typically have low credit limits and high interest rates.*** The limited acceptance can limit the overall utility.

Consider how much money you'll actually be saving over the course of a year. Additionally, judge your ability to pay your balance each month. The answer will tell you if a store card will enhance or challenge your financial situation. It's these little decisions that can have a great impact on your financial well-being.

A traditional credit card may be a better option. Even if you're unable to receive the same discounts, you might be eligible for additional perks, such as airline miles or gift cards. More importantly, it's possible for most consumers to find a credit card with a much lower interest rate and a higher credit limit.

If you have weak credit, a store card can be easier to obtain than many traditional cards. If you have the necessary funds, a secured credit card is another viable option. Ultimately, only you can determine if a store credit card is right for you.

Anchors Away: Finally Break Free from Credit Card Debt

Anyone with credit card debt knows just how challenging it can be. Interest rates are averaging 13 to 16 percent, and it's not easy to get ahead once you have this type of debt.

If you have debts with high interest rates, make paying these a priority. It will bring you a lot of relief to pay them off as soon as possible and be rid of them.

Imagine how much better you'll feel when it's gone. Imagine how much better your finances will look without this debt. Plus, all the money that you're applying to these debts will be available for other purposes when the debt is retired.

These steps will help you eliminate your credit card debt:

1. **Track your spending to the penny for at least a couple of months.** When you're faced with a buying decision, ask yourself if you really need this item. Can you live without it? You're guaranteed to find at least one thing that surprises you if you truly track all of your spending.

2. **Reduce your spending. *After all of that tracking, you can probably see where you're spending more than necessary.*** Trim back and use the extra funds for your debt. Know that you'll eventually end up with a lot more money in your pocket when this debt is gone.

3. **Consider earning some extra income.** Are you overdue for a raise at work? Ask for it. A little overtime or a second job can make a huge difference in knocking down that credit card debt. Try to find something that you will enjoy doing.

4. **Take a look at other credit cards.** Many cards offer interest free account transfers. Keep in mind that *these transfers are frequently only interest-free if you are on time with all of your payments.* One mistake can result in interest being charged on the full balance, even the amount you might have managed to pay down.

    - A card with a lower interest rate is probably out there. A few percent can be significant with a large balance or over a period of time.

5. **Don't be afraid to negotiate.** *You might be able to get your interest rate lowered with a simple phone call.* Your creditor would rather get some interest from you instead of getting nothing. Asking for a better rate costs you nothing.

6. **Build a snowball.** List all your credit card debt from highest interest rate to lowest. Pay the minimums on all the cards except the card with the highest interest rate. Put everything else you can afford toward the highest one. When that one is paid off, repeat the process and focus the highest interest rate card from those that remain.

    - Another version of the snowball is psychologically easier, but is not as efficient. This time, list all the credit cards from lowest balance to highest. Then follow the same procedure, focusing on the debt with the lowest balance.

    - This version is more exciting because you'll pay off a card quicker. However, it's also more expensive since you'll be paying more interest.

    - The most important thing is to start decreasing that debt. *Choosing a process is more important than choosing the best process.* Just get moving forward as soon as possible.

7. **Avoid adding to your debt.** While you're really working at paying off these cards, stop using them. Similarly, don't start using them again after the debt is eliminated.

These simple steps are all anyone really needs to get rid of credit card debt once and for all. While it takes time, the newfound freedom is more than worth it. When it's over, you'll have all that extra money in your pocket to enjoy as you wish.

Get a Handle on Your Debt by Learning How to Deal with Debt Collectors

If debt collectors are pursuing you for payment, you know how frustrating the situation can be. However, ***with knowledge and tact, you can diplomatically navigate the rough waters.***

Try these strategies when you feel like you're drowning in debt and debt collectors:

1. **Take responsibility to become enlightened about your debts.** Rather than ignoring the statements and phone calls, take action to determine how much you owe and to whom. Call the original companies to ask for the balance due. Write down the figures.

    - Inquire whether the debt has been turned over to a collections agency. If it has, record the name of the collection's agency.

2. **Get organized.** Pay special attention to the mail you receive regarding your debts. Save them in a file. Clip together those you believe pertain to a single debt.

3. **Dispute any bills you think you don't owe.** If you receive phone calls or letters about an unfamiliar debt, send a letter to the collections agency to let them know. If you don't owe that money, you can get that cleared up:

   - *Send a copy of your "proof" to the collections agency and the company who thinks you owe them.*

   - For example, perhaps you bought a new washer at the local discount store but when you got home, the washer wouldn't fit in the space you planned. You returned it and received a store credit slip. So include a copy of this credit slip in your communications.

4. **Be polite or at least diplomatic.** Even when a caller is rude or aggressive, confidently choose to hold your tongue and temper. **Let go of the negativity.** It will strengthen your resolve and give you more clarity in determining your best course of action.

5. **Make decisions right away about which bills you'll begin paying.** Let the company know that you plan to begin paying and when.

6. **Be cautious about agreeing to make payments on a large debt.** In some cases, you may be better off by consulting with an attorney rather than paying minimal amounts. Interest and other charges may begin accumulating again as soon as you send your first payment and cost you more money.

7. **Get a short-term second job to earn enough to pay off a debt.** Before you send the money, call the creditor and make an effort to bargain with them to get the original debt down to an amount you can pay. ***Having the money in hand will give you some bargaining power.***

   - For example, perhaps you owe $982 to Company A. You decide to take a second job for six weeks to pay off that debt. At the end of the six weeks, you have $700. Call Company A and tell them you'd like to discuss a settlement of $625 for the entire debt.

8. **Pay off bills to collections agencies with a certified bank check.** Companies can turn in one debt to more than one collection agency, so you'll want to have proof of your payment(s). Also, collections agencies could make an error by misapplying your dollars and then tell the creditor that you didn't pay.

Apply these suggestions and work toward paying off your debts one by one. ***Dispute in writing any claims from companies whom you believe you don't owe.*** Seek legal advice if you need extra support before beginning this process.

Yes, you *can* handle your debts successfully and get back on a positive financial track! Take action now and you can look toward your financial future with optimism.

Signs That You're Carrying Too Much Debt

Debt has practically become a national pastime. The United States and its citizens largely run on credit. While credit can be a great convenience, it can also create major financial challenges. *Carrying too much debt creates a lot of additional costs and stress that are unnecessary.* Anyone who's had a sleepless night because of debt knows how much it can negatively influence your life.

Most of us are used to having a significant amount of debt. But, how much is too much?

Look for these signs that you're carrying too much debt:

1. **You're carrying a credit card balance.** *If you're carrying a credit card balance each month, it's critical to your financial health to pay this debt down.* If you're unable to pay it off, that's a sign that you have too much debt.

2. **You have to use credit cards to pay for everyday items.** Using a credit card to buy food or pay your utility bills is another sign your debt might be out of control. *If you lack the money to pay your routine bills, it might be time to face your debt.*

3. **You're only making the minimum payments on your credit cards.** The minimum payment amounts are designed to keep you paying for an eternity. The less you're paying on the principal, the more you'll be paying in the long run. If you're unable to pay more each month, you're on a slippery slope.

4. **You're regularly making late payments.** Many people think that credit card companies get most of their income from interest, but studies have shown that it's actually the late fees that account for most of their income.

    - Regardless of the type of bill, if your payments are regularly late, you're paying a lot more than necessary. It's also a strong sign that you're carrying too much debt.

5. **You're using payday loans.** Payday loans can be thought of as credit cards for those that are either unable to get a credit card or that have hit their credit limits. ***Payday loans are perhaps the worst loan you can get.***

    - These loan companies get around state usury laws by charging outrageous fees. This is the only way they can legally make as much money as they do.

6. **You're lying to others about your finances.** It's easy to argue that your finances are nobody else's business. If you're lying to family members about your spending habits and your financial well-being, there might be an issue.

7. **You don't have any savings.** One sign of financial health is the ability to save money regularly. If your monthly finances aren't allowing for a regular contribution to your savings account, you're probably playing with fire.

Carrying too much debt is a common occurrence in the United States. Debt can be likened to climbing a mountain with a boulder on your back. ***If you're displaying any of these signs of debt, it's time to do something about it.*** The solution might be as simple as cutting back or as severe as filing for bankruptcy.

Assess your debt and put a plan into place that will ease your financial burden. You'll be glad you did.

Top 5 Causes of Excessive Personal Debt

Excessive debt is the biggest worry of most people. Financial issues are one of the leading contributors to divorce and suicide. ***We are provided with many opportunities to increase our debt but getting out of debt can be especially challenging.*** Think about all the credit card offers and financing opportunities you're faced with every day.

There are many things that create excessive amounts of debt, but the following 5 are among the primary culprits:

1. **Unemployment.** The loss of a job forces many people to rely on consumer debt for survival. Most families lack an emergency fund, and the credit cards are put into action rapidly.

   - Many people fall into the habit of doing just enough work to avoid being fired. ***Put in the time and effort to become an indispensable member of your company.***

   - If you believe that your job is in jeopardy, start looking for a new position! Be proactive.

   - ***Start your emergency fund today.*** If you already have one, ask yourself if it's adequate.

2. **Lack of self-control.** Our society tends to be a little self-indulgent and lacking in discipline. It's largely responsible for the high obesity rates in the United States, as well as the high levels of personal debt. How many items have you purchased in a moment of weakness that you don't ever use or take the time to enjoy?

   - Before making a significant purchase, ask yourself if it's something you need or truly want. If it's merely something you want, ask yourself if it's something you would really enjoy owning. Will you use it?

   - ***Put off significant purchases for a couple of weeks and see if the level of enthusiasm for purchasing it remains.***

   - Remind yourself that $100 invested at 10% is almost $750 in 20 years. That $500 watch or purse is really costing you $3,750 when viewed this way. Over 40 years the cost is almost $5,500 per $100. That $500 item is then $27,300!

3. **Not having a budget or financial goals.** Good things rarely happen without a plan. It's important to have a spending plan and financial goals.

   - ***Create a budget that supports your financial goals.*** Develop habits that support your budget.

   - Regularly review your progress toward your goals and your adherence to your spending plan. When it comes time to make major financial decisions, like purchasing an expensive item, ask yourself if this purchase supports your financial goals.

4. **Excessive or unwise use of credit.** We all have our ways of self-soothing. Some people overeat or drink. Others find healthier ways to cope, like exercising. One of the most damaging ways to make yourself feel better is by shopping. It becomes very easy to use a credit card to temporarily improve your mood by buying something that has caught your eye.

    - *But the long-term pain of excessive debt ultimately replaces that temporary boost.*

5. **Divorce.** Not only can you lose half of your possessions and your net worth, you might be paying your ex-spouse for years to come. You're also likely to be stuck with a big attorney bill.

    - Be careful before jumping into a marriage.
    - *Once conflict begins, seek out professional counseling.*
    - Consider if your situation warrants a pre-nuptial agreement.

Getting out of debt is much more challenging than avoiding it in the first place. *Getting out of debt requires time, a plan, and the necessary discipline to stick to the plan.* But if you can avoid these five primary debt mistakes, avoiding debt will be much easier. If you're already in debt, getting out will be that much easier.

All About Credit Card Delinquency

Even though credit card delinquency has become increasingly common during the past several years, most consumers' understanding of it continues to be lacking.

Too many of us don't know how to avoid or solve this personal financial challenge!

The good news is that once you gain a more complete knowledge of delinquency, dealing with it is relatively straightforward.

When Do You Become Delinquent?

What exactly is credit card delinquency? A credit card customer is delinquent when he fails to make at the least the minimum credit card payment. Delinquency is separated into degrees that indicate how many payments have been missed. These ranges are often referenced in terms of days.

For example, on the day after the first payment is missed, the holder is one day delinquent. After you miss a second payment, the account is deemed to be 30 days delinquent and so on.

Theoretically, **a credit card holder is delinquent after just one missed monthly payment.** On the other hand, delinquency is commonly not reported to the credit bureaus until after two payments in a row have been missed.

What Are the Effects of Delinquency?

Being reported delinquent to the credit bureaus most certainly has a negative impact on credit scores.

Scores could drop as much as 125 points with three consecutive missed payments. Once four payments have been missed, the impact on the credit score is more severe and the account is likely to be sent to collections. Legal action against the cardholder is a real possibility at this point.

How Do You Get Out of Delinquency?

There is a way to stop and get out of delinquency. ***Making a single minimum payment ends the progression of the delinquency*** and keeps the account at the current level of delinquency.

This is crucial, simply because being reported to the credit bureaus 120 days late is much worse than being 90 days late. ***Making even one minimum payment can be an effective strategy*** to keep things from progressing too far.

Once you start trying to make up your past due payments, be careful to avoid these damaging errors:

1. **Making less than the minimum payment.** Unfortunately, making a payment that is less than the minimum doesn't have any effect on the delinquency. So, when you make a small payment, it really doesn't help the situation. This error can easily be avoided; just be sure to only make payments that are greater than or equal to the minimum payment.

2. **Making only one minimum payment.** Frequently, consumers mistake the minimum required payment with the total amount due.

   - ***The total amount due is the amount that needs to be paid in order to bring the account current.*** This amount usually consists of several minimum payments, so it's important to continue making extra payments until the account has been brought current.

Credit Repair After Delinquency

As soon as the account is current, you can start negating the consequences of the delinquency. The more the negative information is covered up with positive information, the less impact the delinquency will have.

Secured credit cards are especially apt for credit betterment. These cards require a deposit to open, and the cards are always approved for this reason. Since the risk is minimal for the credit card company, the fees can be less. Whenever you decide to cancel the card, the deposit is returned.

While credit card delinquency cannot be recovered from overnight, it is possible to suffer no lasting effects in the long-term. Once the delinquency has been rectified, the negative history can be diluted as much as possible.

The key is to be patient and acquire a secured credit card. Using that new card wisely will allow you to be trusted by lenders again. Credit card delinquency is a challenge, but it is a challenge that can be dealt with successfully.

8 Good Reasons to Use a Credit Card

Personal finance gurus spend a lot of energy attempting to prevent us from using credit cards, usually with good reason.

Credit cards are frequently abused and are the cause of a lot of personal debt. ***However, credit cards bring you a lot of advantages as long as you use them wisely.*** In fact, credit cards are frequently a better way to pay for things.

Consider these benefits:

1. **Signup bonuses.** Many credit cards offer significant rewards when used responsibly. For example, consumers with good credit can be approved for credit cards that offer signup bonuses. These bonuses can be worth $50 to $250 or even more. Some credit cards provide points that can be used to redeem rewards like gift cards or airline tickets.

2. **Cash back.** With the right credit card, you can earn from 1-5% back on all your purchases. ***Depending on how much you use it, that can be like getting a raise at work.***

3. **Investment rewards.** Some credit cards, such as the Fidelity Investment Rewards card, give a higher rate of cash back. However, that cash back must be deposited directly into an investment account. This is also nice because it encourages you to invest and save.

4. **Frequent-Flyer miles.** Nearly every airline has at least one credit card offering. The ultimate value of these cards is really determined by the specifics of the card and the airline tickets you actually receive and use. The details can vary so shop around.

5. **Safety.** Using a credit card makes it a lot easier to avoid financial losses due to fraud or unfortunate timing on automatic payments.

    o For example, if you pay your bills with automatic payments directly out of your checking account, these automatic drafts can also potentially result in insufficient funding fees and late payments, which will have a negative effect on your credit score.

    o If your debit card is used fraudulently, your money is taken out of your account instantly. It can also take some time to get your money back. By comparison, **when your credit card is used fraudulently, you don't lose any money;** you simply notify your credit card company and you don't have to pay for those transactions.

6. **Grace period.** Credit card usage gives you time to pay, usually a couple of weeks on the average before any interest kicks in. With a debit card, the money is gone instantly. If you have your money in a high-interest checking account, the amount of interest you will earn can be significantly more over time by paying for your purchases with a credit card.

    o When you put your purchases on your credit card, your money will spend more time in your checking account, where it's earning money for you. If you use a debit card for your purchases, the money is in your account for a much shorter length of time, thus earning less interest.

7. **Insurance.** Most credit cards include a plethora of consumer protections that most people aren't aware of. This includes things like rental car insurance and travel insurance. Some product warranties are also made more advantageous when you pay for the item with your credit card.

8. **Building credit.** If you don't have a credit history or if you need to improve your score, a credit card can help raise your credit score. Obviously, this assumes that you use your card wisely. Debit cards do nothing to help your credit score.

See, credit cards aren't all bad! ***Provided you can use them responsibly, credit cards potentially have a lot to offer.*** So dust off that credit card and put it to good use; just be sure to pay it off in full every month.

Real Estate Strategies

Buying vs. Renting Your Home

Buying or renting a home is a choice that never seems to be settled for certain. It's easy to find experts that claim buying is better; it's also easy to find experts that claim renting is better. **The best idea is to consider all the factors involved and decide which is best for your own circumstances.**

Remember that there are other factors to consider besides money; there are personal and emotional considerations as well. We're going to focus on the financial side, but keep those other factors in mind, too.

1. What is Your Financial Situation?

Can you afford to purchase a home? A down payment and closing costs are going to cost more than the security deposit and first month's rent on a rental. After the initial costs, you still have to be able to afford to stay.

Rental costs tend to be rather fixed. You're not going to have to pay for a new roof or a new furnace. Mortgage payments can be less than rent, but there are the possible repair costs that can always pop up. Rents tend to rise slightly every year, but there are no big surprises.

2. Long-Term Financial Considerations

The main things to consider are equity, tax advantages, and investment potential. These factors do not necessarily guarantee, however, that owning is better than renting, even when looking at purely financial considerations.

3. **Equity.** While making mortgage payments, you build equity in your home. This happens slowly at first, as the bulk of your payment is going to pay the interest on the loan. On the other hand, with renting, you'll never see a penny of the money you'll pay in rent to a landlord; it's gone forever.

   - *If you're only going to be in a home for a short period, renting makes a lot of sense.* You won't have enough time to build any equity in the home unless you got a great deal or the housing market heads for the skies.

4. **Tax advantages.** While rent isn't deductible on your federal income taxes, mortgage interest and property taxes are. Another nice advantage: if you sell your primary residence and make a profit, your gain is exempt from federal taxes (unless you really make a killing). The interest on home equity loans is also deductible in most cases.

   - *Owning a home has several tax advantages, but keep in mind that these tax breaks aren't exactly 'free'.* You will likely pay $1.00 of interest to get back ~$0.33, but you're still losing $0.66. The same goes for your property taxes, and property taxes never go away.

5. **Investment potential.** Paying rent isn't an investment. But if you live in a rent-controlled area, or an area when rents are quite low compared to the cost of home ownership, you could take the extra money you're saving and invest it.

   - A home can be a decent investment, but if you look at the return you get when taking into account all of your costs, it's rarely a great investment. Consider all the money you'll pay in interest, repairs, taxes, and everything else that goes along with owning a home. You'll probably find the return isn't that great.

- Just because your home is probably your largest asset, it doesn't mean it's a great investment. It can be a better investment than rent though, and everyone has to live somewhere.

As you can see, it's not entirely clear-cut whether it's better to rent or own. *In general, it's better to rent in the short-term,* unless the housing market is growing rapidly or you get a fantastic price.

Owning is usually preferred in the long term, but don't kid yourself into believing it's a great investment; in most cases, it's just better than renting.

Do your homework and make a smart choice based on your own situation and how you feel about owning a home. Is it a dream of yours? Do you enjoy the privacy? Do you mind the expense, work and responsibility that go into maintaining a home?

There are many reasons that may lead you to determine that either owning or renting your home is your best choice.

Introduction to Budgeting for First Time Mortgagees

Congratulations on buying your first home! This is surely a great achievement for you and the rewards can be very exciting. ***As a homeowner, you have equity that's solid.*** There's so much you can accomplish now that you have this asset under your belt.

What you'll now realize, however, is that your bank account has started to behave erratically! You're seeing money moving out of your account faster than ever before. Or so it seems.

What you're experiencing is a clear case of a budgeting dilemma for a first time mortgagee. It's completely normal to feel like you've lost some control over your finances now that you're a home owner.

The good news is that you can learn how to budget all over again. It's certainly going to be necessary for a positive mortgaging experience.

1. **Make your mortgage payment first.** ***If you want to continue to hold on to your home, ensure you pay your mortgage on time!*** Remember the home is yours and you want to keep it that way. As soon as you get your pay check, withdraw the amount you need for your mortgage.

    - A great idea is to set up an automatic payment to the mortgage lender from your bank account. That way, you won't have to worry about remembering to make the payment each month. ***Sure, things come up, but defaulting on your mortgage payment could mean not having a roof over your head!***

    - Avoid using the equity in your home as a cash advance. Stay as far from additional debt as possible.

2. **Prioritize other expenses.** With the mortgage payment out of the way, you now have to manage all the other expenses. Now that you have a mortgage, your priorities may likely shift.

    - All expenses related to the new home are important. However, you need to ask yourself if all of them are necessary right now. ***Focus on the recurring monthly expenses that contribute to a comfortable dwelling.***

    - Social time is certainly important, especially when it comes to maintaining your sanity! But try to cut down on entertainment expenses. Instead of going to the movies 3 times per week, go out once and rent a movie twice.

3. **Schedule home improvement.** As a new homeowner, you'll have the ongoing desire to make the home more beautiful. ***While your pride of place is admirable, it's important to let better senses rule!***

    - Make a list of all your home improvement needs and wants.

    - Prioritize them, with the ones that make the home safe and livable taking precedence over the others.

    - Put a schedule in place for accomplishing everything, and tie that into the associated expenses. Your aim should be to commit the same amount of money each month to home improvement.

    - If there's something you aren't able to afford this month, simply leave the rest until next month.

4. **Make saving a priority.** With all that can happen as a new homeowner, it's more important than ever to set aside money in your savings account. Major repairs sometimes need to be taken care of immediately.

- Have the discipline to put aside untouchable savings. That way, there'll be something for rainy days!

Mortgaging a home for the first time can leave you jaded if you aren't able to budget effectively. ***Pay close attention to the spending of every dollar.*** Once you've mastered that, you can feel comfortable knowing the financial responsibilities related to your home are well taken care of!

Practical Tips for the First-Time Home Buyer

The decision to go from renter to homeowner is a big one. When you own your own home there are a lot of responsibilities, but there are also a lot of benefits.

Buying a home for the first time can be intimidating. The reason it's daunting is because, for most individuals, it's the single largest purchase they're ever going to make.

To ease your fears and ensure you make the best choices, there are some things that every first-time home buyer ought to know.

Follow this advice to ensure your home buying experience is successful:

1. **Determine what you'll be able to afford.** Before you start house hunting, figure out exactly how much you can afford to spend.

    - Make a budget by taking your monthly income and then subtracting all of your monthly expenses. This will tell you how much you can afford to spend on your mortgage payments.

    - ***As a general rule of thumb, it's recommended that you spend no more than 28% of your income on housing costs.***

2. **Determine what your monthly housing costs will be.** Your monthly housing costs won't just include your mortgage payments, but also your property taxes and homeowner's insurance.

    - To figure out what your mortgage payments will be, you can get preapproved for a loan. The lender will be able to tell you what the interest rate on your loan will be and what the monthly payments will come out to.

    - ***Before you buy a house, you can ask what the current property taxes are, so you have an idea.*** Sometimes, your property taxes are added on to your mortgage payment.

    - To figure out how much you might have to spend on homeowner's insurance, you can contact different insurance providers for quotes. Shop around for the best rates!

3. **Get in touch with a real estate agent.** After you've done your homework, it's a good idea to use a realtor to help you find the perfect house. If you decide to go house hunting on your own without a realtor, you'll be limiting your options.

    - ***A realtor can quickly and easily look up all of the properties that are available in a particular geographical area and price range.***

    - They can also get you in to see vacant homes which you're unable to do on your own.

    - A realtor will also help you navigate through the mountain of paperwork that has to be filled out when purchasing a home.

Keep These Tips in Mind While House Hunting

1. **Location is key!** Let your realtor know what's important to you and they'll show you houses in a fitting location.

    - If you have health concerns, you may want to buy a house near a hospital or your doctor. You're probably looking for a house near a school if you have young children. Perhaps you want to be near restaurants and shopping. ***Figure out your location needs and communicate them.***

2. **Bring a digital camera and a notepad.** It's important to gather information about each house, so you can go back and review it later. You want to be sure of your choice before buying a house.

    - Make notes about each house you visit, jotting down the things you like or don't like. You can even rate each house on a scale of 1 to 10.

    - With a digital camera, you can take lots of pictures of the houses you look at. This will help you remember some details after a long day of house hunting.

    - After looking at a number of homes, go back to your top choices for a second look.

At this point you're ready to make an offer to buy your first house. Your real estate agent will give you some advice about how much to offer, and then they'll deliver your offer to the listing agent. If all goes well, it won't be long until you're moving into your first home.

Should You Pay Off Your Mortgage Early?

If you're paying a mortgage, at one time or another you've probably thought about what it would be like to pay it off. You've likely dreamed about living the life you desire, unfettered by the ball and chain of having to pay your loan payment every month.

Before you make a decision, however, take a close look at your financial options to determine if it really would be wise to pay off your loan early. ***In some situations, it's better not to pay it off.***

Consider these reasons, both for and against, an early payoff in your situation.

Benefits of Paying Off Your Mortgage

1. **You'll save big on interest.** Depending on where you are time-wise in the term of the loan, you stand to save literally thousands of dollars that you would have paid in interest over the life of your loan.

2. **You won't have the monthly stress of a house payment.** This can be a great relief!

3. **As retirement approaches, paying your house off means you won't have to struggle** with house payments on a reduced income.

4. **You'll have hundreds of dollars to spend or save monthly.** It's empowering to know that whether you want to take a couple more trips a year or concentrate on saving for the kids' educations, you'll have money to put aside for it.

5. **Your confidence about your financial situation will increase.** After all, if you pay off your mortgage early, ***you're likely doing something right with your budget.*** You have a lot to be proud of!

Why You Might Not Want To Pay Off Your Mortgage

Taking all of the above into account, sometimes you can still come out ahead without paying off your mortgage early.

Here are some reasons why:

1. **Paying interest has its advantages.** With mortgage rates being so low now, you might be paying only 3 or 4% on your mortgage. Yet you might find an investment that pays you a 10% return. ***So you would make more money if you used your extra funds to make a higher rate of interest from an investment rather than pay down your mortgage.***

   - Bear in mind that if you're getting an income tax deduction on your mortgage interest, that interest is costing you even less overall.

2. **Keeping your dollars in hand may be wiser.** Paying off your mortgage in one lump sum might not work in your best interest. Doing so doesn't increase your net worth because you'll have less cash.

   - Also, paying all your cash into your house means you have substantially fewer liquid dollars. You'd have to sell or refinance your house to get your cash back if you need it. ***It's unwise to use all your cash to pay off your mortgage,*** especially if you could be earning interest on it.

3. **Avoid taking cash out of your 401(k) to pay off your house,** especially if you're less than age 59-1/2 because of the extra penalty. Plus, all the money you take out is taxed at your ordinary income rate.

4. **Paying off loans with higher interest rates first makes more sense.** ***It's smarter to pay off a higher interest debt than your mortgage, if your mortgage has a lower interest rate.*** Answering the question of whether to pay off your mortgage early takes some deliberation.

The Top 6 Home Improvements with the Best Return

Many home improvements are little more than money pits. Some improvements don't even appeal to many homebuyers. Over $200 billion is spent every year on home renovations, but how many of those dollars are spent in a way that truly improves the value of the home?

Many people are shocked at how little their improvements added to the sales price of their home.

Some home improvements can boost your home's resale value and the level of comfort you experience while you're still living there. Unfortunately, there are other improvements that can cost thousands of dollars and provide little to no return.

These home improvements are likely to pay off better than any other:

1. **New siding.** From an investment standpoint, fiber cement siding is the way to go. Vinyl siding can crack over time, and aluminium siding ultimately ends up with dents. Even with professional installation, this is still a cost-effective upgrade.

2. **New front door.** ***Fiberglass doors are very expensive, but a mid-range steel door looks great and can easily be painted to match your home.*** The simpler the door, the lower the cost. But steel doors are so inexpensive that you can afford to pick up something nice.

3. **Garage door replacement.** While no one gets excited about replacing their garage door, some jobs just need to be done. A mid-quality garage door will add to your curb appeal and improve the functionality and sales price of your home. Garage doors are easily painted, too.

4. **Wood deck.** Nearly everyone loves to sit out on a deck when the weather permits. It's the perfect transition between indoors and the outside. It effectively adds living space, and the material costs are quite low.

    - If you're handy with a circular saw, tape measure, and hammer or drill, you might be able to install your deck yourself.

5. **New windows.** *Newer windows eliminate drafts, reduce radiant heat in the summer, and provide much better insulation than older style windows.* They look great, too! While windows can be expensive, the payback is quite good. Compare costs and the amount of insulation. The utility savings can be impressive.

6. **Fresh interior paint.** Although paint is relatively inexpensive, the labor can be pricey. Fortunately, anyone can tackle this task on their own. You'll save a lot of money and your house will look great. Take your time and you can do a great job.

    - Stick to neutral colors that everyone can accept. If you'll be selling soon, now isn't the time for unusual colors.

Unless you're planning on staying in your home for an extended period of time, it's important to consider how your improvements will affect the sales price of your home.

Many improvements do little to increase the value of your home. However, if you'll be in your home for many years, it's completely reasonable to place a priority on the enjoyment you'll receive from the upgrade.

Being the nicest house on the block might be great for the ego, but it's hard on the pocketbook. Avoid adding features to your home that aren't appropriate for your neighborhood. If you're in a middle-class setting, remodeling projects common to luxury homes are likely to be financial disasters.

A little forethought will ensure that your home improvements make your home more attractive, livable, and valuable. **_Research the costs and expected payback of any improvements you're considering._** Remember to examine the cost of labor. Nearly any project can provide a nice return, especially if you can do the work yourself.

Tax Tips for Homeowners

You may already know that you can deduct the mortgage interest you pay on your home, but what other tax advantages are lurking in that house?

One of the biggest challenges of owning a home is dealing with the tax laws, especially those around points and cost basis. Just a little bit of knowledge can really clear up these frequently confusing terms. Here's the scoop on mortgage basis points and how they're used in your home's value, cost basis, and tax burden.

What are Points?

Points are fees that you pay in order to enter into a mortgage. ***Points are considered to be prepaid interest, and as such, you can deduct them.*** The issue is, can you deduct the full amount up front, or must you divide your deductions out over the life of the loan?

You can deduct all the points the first year if all of the following are true:

- The loan is used to purchase or build your primary home.
- Paying points is customary in your area.
- The points aren't paid for appraisal fees, title fees, property taxes, or similar fees.
- You didn't borrow the money to pay the points.
- The points were based on a percentage of the loan and that fact is easy to see.

Cost Basis

Cost basis is the original value of an asset for tax purposes. The cost basis is quite easy to calculate; it is simply the price you paid for the home plus any capital improvements that have been made. Then you would subtract any seller-paid points, depreciation, and losses.

Capital improvements would be anything that increases the home's value. Capital improvements would include such things as swimming pools and adding a room.

Understanding the Tax Burden When You Sell

If you owned the home (and lived in it) for at least two out of the last 5 years, you most likely don't owe any tax at all. A single person doesn't pay tax on capital gains of less than $250,000; for married couples the limit is $500,000. So as a married couple, you could purchase a home for $100,000 and sell it for $600,000 and not owe any tax on the proceeds.

There are circumstances under which the two-year requirement is waived, such as health issues, divorce, change of employment, and more.

In these cases, the amount of the exemption is based on the number of months the home was lived in. So if you were single and lived there for 12 months, you would be entitled to an exemption of $125,000, or half of the deduction allowed if you had lived there the required two years.

Inherited Property

The cost basis on inherited property is the market value *at the time of the owner's death.*

This is great, because it doesn't matter how much your grandmother paid for her home back in 1960. If you inherited the home she paid $20,000 for, and it's now worth $175,000 (when she died), you would not owe any tax on the proceeds even if you were to sell the home immediately.

While it's likely that the related tax laws will change again (they always do), it's always a good idea to understand your home's cost basis and your potential tax liability. Sooner or later the information may be pertinent to your tax situation, so keep abreast of the tax implications and deductions for your home.

What Does Renter's Insurance Cover?

Consider these attributes of coverage with renter's insurance:

1. **Loss of property.** Renter's insurance will cover the loss of your personal possessions in the same situations that your homeowner's policy covered. This will include occurrences such as fire, theft, storm damage, and water damage.

    - *Be aware that certain types of property like jewelry, high-end electronics, and antiques may require specific coverage with a rider.*

2. **Add a rider for earthquakes, floods, or hurricanes.** As with homeowner's policies, damage from earthquake and flood typically are not covered. Separate coverage or a rider is required if these are relevant to your geographical area.

    - Inquire about damage from hurricanes if those can be an issue where you live. After a hurricane, you may find it difficult to collect, so ensure you know what you're getting up front.

3. **Actual replacement cost vs. cash value.** When looking at policies, understand whether the policy covers the replacement cost or the cash value.

    - If only the cash value is covered, for example, you won't receive enough to fund the replacement of your 10-year old leather couch.

    - Purchasing a policy that provides the actual replacement cost will cover what it really costs you to replace your property, but the premiums will be higher.

4. **Policy limits.** Know the limits on the coverage within your policy. Some policies have a cap on the total payout, too.

5. **Liability.** Renter's policies usually cover some liability.

    - For example, if someone slips in your apartment and breaks his arm, you're likely to be covered.

    - You may also be covered if your dog bites someone, but certain breeds are frequently excluded, so be sure to check on these restrictions if you have a dog.

    - Any accidental damage you cause to the building is also usually covered. So if you trip and put your shoulder through the dry wall, your insurance should cover the cost to repair the wall.

Cost

The cost of coverage is usually quite low - often no more than $100 per year.

The factors that determine the cost include the amount of the deductible, your location, and your specific needs beyond the basics. Discounts are usually available for having safety features like burglar alarms, smoke detectors, and fire extinguishers. Having additional policies with the same insurance company can also reduce your cost.

You can lower your premiums by having a sprinkler system for fire, dead-bolt locks, only non-smokers in the household, electronic payments, and a good credit rating. Electronic payments require less labor to process, so many companies charge more if you mail yours. The other items are risk management issues. A non-smoking household is much less likely to have a fire.

Before you sign up for a specific policy, ***sit down with your insurance agent and see what other premium discounts might apply to your situation.*** You could save yourself a bunch of cash.

Document Your Property

Make a list of all your belongings, with photos, before you get your policy. It would be an even better idea to make a video. Store your list or video in a private location online or in a safe deposit box at your bank. Keeping the video in the video camera won't help you much if the camera gets stolen or destroyed in a fire. The same goes for a list on your computer.

Becoming a renter instead of a homeowner doesn't mean you no longer need insurance. Your possessions still need to be insured and you still have potential liabilities. Because of this, renter's insurance makes sense. It brings you a lot of peace of mind for only a little money!

Common Real Estate Investing Mistakes

Although real estate may seem like a sure bet for anyone, many investors make the same few mistakes. ***Eliminate these errors from your investing activities and you'll be well on your way to accumulating the wealth you desire.***

Avoid These Mistakes

1. **Poor research.** Most of us do a lot of research when we plan our vacations or purchase a new television. If you were buying a TV worth 100k, you can bet you'd do even more research! Well, you should be doing that when you purchase a piece of real estate, too.

2. **Inadequate financing.** Real estate investors frequently like to wheel and deal, and their deals can have a lot of moving parts. Balloon payments, interest-only payments, owner financing, subject-to, and many others are commonplace.

   - To make a deal happen, we can get carried away doing everything in our power. Getting a great price doesn't always justify the deal if the financing is inadequate. Are you sure that you can unload the property or get other financing before that balloon payment comes due?

3. **Trying to do everything yourself.** Though every real estate investor attempts this at one time or another, ***you have little chance at success all by yourself.*** A great investor will have, at a minimum, a real estate agent, attorney, title company, inspector, handyman, and insurance agent – all on speed dial.

   - You may not always need them, but they should already be in place, and you shouldn't hesitate to call them if you do want their services. Use your experts to your full advantage.

4. **Paying too much.** This one is certainly related to doing enough research. Real estate deals primarily sink, or swim based on price. If you pay too much, not much can be done to rectify the situation.

   - Beginning investors are more likely to mentally fudge the numbers a little bit to make a deal happen. But if the repairs run high, and the price they can sell for is lower than expected, then overpaying in the first place can be disastrous. Do your research and your math and ***stick to your numbers.***

5. **Not estimating expenses accurately.** This is like paying too much. Many investors will look at repairs and think to themselves, *"Everyone is saying it will take $20,000 to fix, but I'm sure I can get it done for $14,000."* But what if it really takes $23,500? That's part of the reason getting the property at the right price is so important.

   - The other aspect of this mistake is not accounting for all expenses. The costs of landscaping, lawn mowing, insurance, utilities, property taxes, and new appliances can really add up in a hurry. ***Be realistic with your repair planning*** and take careful notes of all your possible expenses.

Real estate investing is a relatively simple business, but mistakes can create massive challenges in a hurry.

Every seasoned investor has made all these mistakes. The best investors just make them less often than everyone else. In any housing market, there are moneymaking opportunities, so don't let these mistakes slow you down!

Beware of These 5 Common Foreclosure Scams

Everyone that owns a home values the ability to go home at the end of a hard day and close the door on the rest of the world.

Our home is our sanctuary and a big part of the reason many of us go to work every day in the first place. Unfortunately, financial challenges can put home ownership at risk; after all, your house is usually your collateral for your mortgage.

Unfortunately, there are many companies that attempt to prey on those that are in danger of losing their home. While not all companies are disreputable, many are. Let's look at the most common scams out there.

Common Foreclosure Scams:

1. **Equity Stripping.** In this scam, a mortgage lender is well aware of your challenging financial situation and pushes you to get a larger mortgage to pay off the original mortgage. This larger mortgage has even larger monthly payments than original mortgage.

   - Of course, it's only a matter of time before you have difficulty making the payments. ***The new lender then swoops in and takes your home.*** You won't have much, if any, equity left because the new loan was large enough to swallow it all up. The equity has effectively been 'stripped.'

2. **Lender Scams.** Your lender may offer to refinance your home with an interest-only payment plan. This can be great, for a while. Your payments will be much lower at first. Eventually, however, there is likely to be a large balloon payment due.

    - Many people won't be able to make the balloon payment or be able to get another refinance to stop the new foreclosure. While this is not technically a scam, ***it usually turns a bad situation much worse.***

3. **Equity Skimming.** In this instance, a buyer will convince you to sign your property over to him in exchange for making your payments. The buyer will then rent out your property and start collecting rent. The buyer will not make your payments as promised and the lender will foreclose.

    - If you have a significant amount of equity, the buyer will flip the property to another buyer at a higher price and keep all the profits. Instead of falling for this, if you're in danger of losing your home to foreclosure, ***sell it yourself and profit from your equity.***

4. **Loan Flipping.** Here your lender will encourage you to refinance your loan, with the enticement of getting extra cash for home repairs or a vacation. Shortly after you refinance, they will hit you up with another offer to refinance.

    - The additional fees and cost associated with the loans will be significant and greater than any benefits you receive. It will be even more difficult to make your payments. ***This is simply a way for a lender to extract more money from you before they foreclose on your home.***

5. **Phony Loan Transactions.** An unscrupulous lender refinances your loan and provides documentation that gives the appearance of bringing your loan current. Sometimes, these documents can transfer your home's title to the company.

It's normal to be stressed and searching for solutions when your home is at stake. Many unscrupulous people are aware that you might be desperate and agree to anything that looks like a lifeline. They can discover your situation from public records. Be aware of the common scams that are out there and look out for your best interests.

There is frequently a solution available, but the potential solutions above are unlikely to be the answer you're looking for.

How to Calculate ROI for Real Estate Investments

ROI or *Return on Investment* is a term to describe how much you profit from an investment. **It is the percentage of money made on an investment after all the costs associated with that investment are subtracted.** So, if you invested $10 and earned $1, your ROI would be 10%, assuming you get your original $10 back.

The basic equation is:

$$\frac{\text{(Gain} - \text{Investment Cost)}}{\text{Your Cost}} \times 100\%$$

Let's look at the two basic methods of applying this equation to real estate investments:

1. **The Out-of-Pocket Method**

    Suppose you purchased a house for $100,000. The needed rehab was $60,000 and the eventual selling price was $200,000. Let's also assume that the investor only had to come up with a $10,000 down payment and the rehab costs.

    The ROI would be:

    $$\frac{(\$200,000 - \$160,000)}{\$70,000} \times 100\% = \mathbf{\sim 57\%}$$

2. **The Cost Method**

   Let's use the same imaginary situation, but the investor paid for everything with his own money.

   The equity in the property is $40,000 (200,000 – 100,000 – 60,000= $40,000).

   The ROI would be $40,000 / $160,000 = **25%** (A 40k profit on 160k spent).

The first method allows for the use of leverage, so it might seem better to borrow as much as you can. But consider that that actual amount of money you would make would be greater in # 2, since there wouldn't be any costs associated with the loan. So your rate of return might be lower, but the number of dollars in your pocket would be greater.

Which method you choose is up to you. The point is to stick to one method when comparing different prospective investments. ***ROI can be an excellent tool to determine which deal is better than another.***

Other Considerations

Don't be concerned with equity in your calculations; *it's better to be concerned with the amount of money you are left with at the end.* You need to consider all your expenses, such as:

- Property taxes that you have to pay
- Insurance while you're holding the property
- Utilities
- Interest on any loans
- Closing costs, both to buy and to sell the property
- Real estate commissions when you sell
- Mowing the grass until the property sells
- Appraisal and inspection costs
- Costs for repairs – both materials and labor

The real estate shows you see on TV rarely address all these costs. All they talk about is the purchase price, cost of repairs, and the selling price. As you can see, repair costs are only one of many costs that you may be responsible for. Those shows have nothing to do with reality. *Be sure you're subtracting all your expected costs when you do your calculations.*

Also consider time. Is a 40% return in 12 months better than a 20% return in 12 weeks? In most cases, no, it is not. Just be sure to consider the time period when you're making comparisons.

Also consider cash flow. In the case of an apartment building, your 'gain' would be the rents that you collect over the course of a year. But be sure to include a vacancy rate in your calculations. There are also greater costs associated with owning rental properties: repairs in the middle of the night, painting between tenants, advertising, carpeting, landscaping, and more.

Getting an accurate ROI estimate really isn't possible in real estate. You never truly know your future selling price or how long it will take. Repair estimates can be off as well.

That's why *it's important to estimate high on your costs and low on the income.* Be conservative and you'll always be pleasantly surprised in the end!

Stress-Free Vacation Strategies

7 Tips to Save Money on Your Next Vacation

The travel options most of us are exposed to are expensive. It's unlikely that you'll see many advertisements for budget vacations. ***The travel destinations you see in colorful brochures, high-end magazines, and on television are run by high-profit travel companies.*** While those vacations are a possibility, there are more economical options to consider.

Many people manage to travel the world on a budget of $50 or less per day!

Take advantage of these strategies and save money on your next vacation:

1. **Try the shoulder season.** Hitting Europe in the summer and Aruba in the winter might be ideal. However, you can save a lot of money by traveling just before or after peak seasons. The costs are lower and the weather is still good. It's also less crowded and more peaceful.

2. **Bid for your hotel room.** Most travelers are aware of websites like Priceline.com and Hotwire.com. But, it's challenging to know if you're getting the best deal.

    - Betterbidding.com can provide actual bidding information and advice for the popular bidding websites. You can find out the average room rate and compare. Then, you'll know with certainty if you're bidding too little or too much.

3. **Wait until the last minute.** *While airfares go through the roof close to the travel date, many other travel-related services, like cruises and tours, tend to drop in price.*

    - Why is that? Who flies at the last minute? Typically people on business-related travel. This group of travelers isn't as price conscious.

    - Cruises and tours mostly have fixed costs, so they get all the money upfront. There's little reason to send out a cruise ship with empty rooms. Leaving those rooms vacant gets them zero dollars, so they'd rather sell trips at a discount to bring in more income.

4. **Plan your meals.** It's easy to spend a lot of money on food, especially if you have a large family. Find discount coupons and deals ahead of time. Decide where you're going to eat before starting on your journey.

    - Remember that you can cook for yourself, too, even on vacation, with some advance planning. An electric skillet can save you a lot when you're on vacation!

5. **Travel light.** Airlines like to give the impression of lower fares, but by now you likely know the truth. They charge for everything else that used to be free. And bags cost a fortune. Some airlines charge for any checked luggage. Plus, overweight bags can cost you literally *hundreds* of extra dollars before you even board the plane for your trip!

6. **If you're taking a road trip, consider your gas consumption.** *There are many rewards programs that can help you save money on gas.* If you have a smart phone, you can find apps to assist you with finding the best gas prices on your route. Many gift cards give additional discounts on gasoline, as well.

7. **Find free entertainment.** Most cities have some sort of free entertainment just about every day of the week. Many museums offer free admission one day a week. Get online and see what's happening where you're vacationing.

A budget vacation doesn't have to feel like you're skimping. It simply requires some creative planning. ***With a concerted effort, you can have your greatest vacation ever, without breaking the bank.***

Use these tips and your own ideas to save money while giving your family a vacation to remember.

What If... You Had a Vacation with No Bills?

Do the sweet memories of your vacation tarnish a bit when you start getting the credit card bills for it the month after you return home, or as you spend a year paying off your trip from *last* year? Imagine how differently you would feel if there were no bills to come home to!

The best way to steer clear of anxiety and guilt is to save for your trip before ever heading out the door. This will result in a more enjoyable vacation because you'll already have the money set aside and won't have to worry.

It's easy to save for a vacation if you set a goal, cut back on your spending, and save money on a regular basis.

Follow these tips to budget and save for your next vacation:

1. **Agree on a goal.** Get together with the family and agree on a vacation destination. Saving is rarely exciting, but once it's attached to an objective, it becomes tolerable.

2. **Develop a vacation budget.** If you want to save painlessly, a budget helps. Based on your destination, create a reasonable budget. Be certain to include everything. If someone needs to care for your dog and cut your grass, include it. Take the time to be accurate.

3. **Calculate a weekly goal.** Divide your budget by the number of weeks until your vacation. That's how much you need to save each week. ***Saving weekly makes it easier to get back on track if you miss a target.*** If you're an entire month behind, it's more challenging to get caught up.

4. **Find ways to "create" some excess money.** Make a detailed list of your monthly expenses and see where you can cut back. Everyone buys things that are "wants" rather than needs.

    - Food is one area where most families spend too much. Avoid eating out more than necessary and make an effort to shop more economically. Packaged foods tend to be more expensive than the healthier alternatives.

    - *Consider ditching your landline or any other service you don't really use.* You, your spouse, and maybe even your children have cell phones. Do you need a landline, too? What about that gym membership? Are you using it regularly?

    - Look at the loans you're carrying. If you haven't checked the interest rates lately, you might be able to save a significant amount by refinancing.

5. **Put away the money you save on cutting back.** It's one thing to cut your cell phone bill or loan payment down. It's another to actually take that $50 and set it aside so it won't be spent. Create a savings account and simply transfer the money you've saved into it each week.

    - Consider having some money automatically transferred into a "vacation savings account" each month.

    - *Try throwing all your change into a jar at the end of each day and deposit it into your vacation account whenever it gets full.*

6. **Assess your progress.** Regularly check on the status of your savings. Look at the calendar and see how you're doing in regards to your savings target. ***Then, make any necessary changes.***

Saving for a vacation can be easy and painless. It all starts with a goal and a budget. With those two items in place, you can determine how much you need to save and implement your plan. Have the best vacation ever without having to worry about spending outside your means!

All-Inclusive Vacations Can Save You Money

Most of us carefully plan our vacations to fit our paychecks. Somehow, though, in spite of all of our best intentions, vacations always seem to cost more than we expect. We go each time with a plan in hand, and each time, we come back wondering where all the money went.

Budgeting for the big things like travel and lodging is pretty straight forward. ***Smaller expenses are usually the cause of unplanned spending.*** Entertainment, food, and drinks are more difficult to plan well for, since these items can be rather spontaneous in nature.

But you can avoid the overspending and still feel like you're treating yourself well. One possible solution is an all-inclusive vacation. Let's have a look at this type of package, and make this the year when you come back with both happy memories *and* a few bucks in your wallet.

What's Included

All-inclusive vacations can really help you stay within your budget. **You pay a fixed rate for all the essentials.** As long as you don't spend money outside the resort, you're all set. If you prefer not to worry about money while vacationing, these types of packages can be ideal.

All-inclusive resorts are really the equivalent of an insurance policy. You pay a set amount in exchange for having access to everything you need, when you need it.

What's Not Included

However, *you won't have the same level of freedom.* Unless you want to pull out your wallet again, you'll have to confine your food, beverages, and entertainment to the resort. Also, if you decide you don't like the resort you've chosen, you're stuck with what you've got.

Vacationing the more traditional way, you can always check out and head down the street to another hotel if you're not pleased. Only you know how much that flexibility is worth to you.

Also, you've already paid for the package, even if you don't use it. Be sure you're going to get your money's worth. For example, if your idea of vacation is sitting on the beach all day and eating one meal a day, you're going to be paying for a lot more than you're using with an all-inclusive package. In this case, you might be better off with a traditional vacation.

Consider these ideas to minimize your potential risk when booking an all-inclusive resort:

1. **Look for amenities that suit you.** Consider what you want to eat. Do hotdogs and potato chips sound good to you? Maybe you want a vacation that includes gourmet food in a nice restaurant setting.

    - Some less-expensive places will only provide water, soda, and a few more beverages. Do you want to have access to mixed drinks and fine wine? Many resorts will not include alcoholic beverages unless you pay extra.
    - Do you enjoy the types of entertainment they offer?
    - How is the customer service?

2. **Consider the quality of the accommodations.** Some resorts are bare bones, while others are extremely plush. Be sure you're getting the best combination of what you can afford and what you want.

3. **Do your homework.** *Researching the quality of the resort is the most important task you can undertake before you book your vacation.* In the Internet age, reviews and suggestions are easy to find. Low-quality establishments have a harder time hiding than ever before.

All in all, an all-inclusive package can be a great way to put a cap on your vacation spending. There are no surprises, and you can eat and drink without worrying about budget or about how much money you have left.

Vacations commonly result in overspending, but with an all-inclusive package, you can stay in charge of your finances even as you play. Start doing your research now; an all-inclusive vacation might be just the ticket this year.

Retirement and Estate Planning Strategies

Renter's Insurance and Retirees

Does your house feel empty and oversized now that your kids have homes of their own? Maybe now is the time to move to a condo or apartment. You'd be free of mowing the grass, cleaning out of the gutters, and shoveling the driveway. And perhaps best of all: no more property taxes!

If you decide to downsize your residence and rent instead of own, you'll no longer need homeowner's insurance. Even so, **you'll still have stuff to insure, and renter's insurance is your financial solution.**

What Does Renter's Insurance Cover?

Consider these attributes of coverage with renter's insurance:

1. **Loss of property.** Renter's insurance will cover the loss of your personal possessions in the same situations that your homeowner's policy covered. This will include occurrences such as fire, theft, storm damage, and water damage.

    - *Be aware that certain types of property like jewelry, high-end electronics, and antiques may require specific coverage with a rider.*

2. **Add a rider for earthquakes, floods, or hurricanes.** As with homeowner's policies, damage from earthquake and flood typically are not covered. Separate coverage or a rider is required if these are relevant to your geographical area.

- Inquire about damage from hurricanes if those can be an issue where you live. After a hurricane, you may find it difficult to collect, so ensure you know what you're getting up front.

3. **Actual replacement cost vs. cash value.** When looking at policies, understand whether the policy covers the replacement cost or the cash value.

- If only the cash value is covered, for example, you won't receive enough to fund the replacement of your 10-year old leather couch.

- Purchasing a policy that provides the actual replacement cost will cover what it really costs you to replace your property, but the premiums will be higher.

4. **Policy limits.** Know the limits on the coverage within your policy. Some policies have a cap on the total payout, too.

5. **Liability.** Renter's policies usually cover some liability.

- For example, if someone slips in your apartment and breaks his arm, you're likely to be covered.

- You may also be covered if your dog bites someone, but certain breeds are frequently excluded, so be sure to check on these restrictions if you have a dog.

- Any accidental damage you cause to the building is also usually covered. So if you trip and put your shoulder through the dry wall, your insurance should cover the cost to repair the wall.

Cost

The cost of coverage is usually quite low - often no more than $100 per year.

The factors that determine the cost include the amount of the deductible, your location, and your specific needs beyond the basics. Discounts are usually available for having safety features like burglar alarms, smoke detectors, and fire extinguishers. Having additional policies with the same insurance company can also reduce your cost.

You can lower your premiums by having a sprinkler system for fire, dead-bolt locks, only non-smokers in the household, electronic payments, and a good credit rating. Electronic payments require less labor to process, so many companies charge more if you mail yours. The other items are risk management issues. A non-smoking household is much less likely to have a fire.

Before you sign up for a specific policy, **sit down with your insurance agent and see what other premium discounts might apply to your situation.** You could save yourself a bunch of cash.

Document Your Property

Make a list of all your belongings, with photos, before you get your policy. It would be an even better idea to make a video. Store your list or video in a private location online or in a safe deposit box at your bank. Keeping the video in the video camera won't help you much if the camera gets stolen or destroyed in a fire. The same goes for a list on your computer.

Becoming a renter instead of a homeowner doesn't mean you no longer need insurance. Your possessions still need to be insured and you still have potential liabilities. Because of this, renter's insurance makes sense. It brings you a lot of peace of mind for only a little money!

Top Reasons to Revise Your Will

Perhaps you, like many others, believe that once your will has been drawn up, that's the end of the process. While wills have never been anyone's idea of fun, it's important to review your will on a regular basis. **There are many reasons to pull out your will and give it a thorough review.**

Let's examine the most common reasons:

1. **New family members.** In general, if a will is worded properly, any children that are born after the will has been signed will be entitled to the same share of the estate as the pre-existing children. Even so, if you have a new child, check with your attorney just to be sure everything is worded according to your wishes.

   - Also consider how your wishes might change based on other new people in your life. What if you re-connect with a family member? What if you make a new best friend? Maybe one of them would be the person to take good care of your boat when you're gone. **Consider all new people who've entered your life since you signed your will.**

2. **Moving.** States have different laws regarding estate taxes and how property is treated. So if you move from one state to another, there may be some major issues that need to be examined. Consult your attorney anytime you move to a new state as this can have significant ramifications.

3. **A windfall.** A large increase in your wealth may require another look at your will. Again, this depends on your state. Some states have monetary limits for certain types of inheritance items. ***Creating a trust might be the right move for you now.***

    - With your new wealth, you may also have a greater degree of flexibility to take advantage of certain tax shelters. And you might be considering being more generous regarding who's included in your will.

4. **Divorce.** Most of us aren't interested in leaving anything to our ex-spouses. If you've gotten divorced since your will was drawn up, it's time to talk to your attorney. A proper and thorough revision will reduce the likelihood of the will being contested. Consider the fact that if you don't change this document, ***your ex could end up with everything!***

5. **Death**. If your spouse or only child passes away, your will should undergo a thorough review. This event may radically change how you wish to distribute your assets. Back-up recipients are usually specified within a will, but it never hurts to take another look.

6. **Change of heart.** Most wills are drafted by people who are still quite young. As you age, however, ***your wishes may change.*** Maybe you were very close to your brother at one point, but haven't spoken to him in the last five years.

    - Additionally, as some people age, they become more involved with charitable organizations. Maybe you'll have the desire to include such a group in your will.

Your will we most likely not be a static document throughout your life. As your circumstances, family, and social connections change, some modifications will likely need to be made.

4 Critical Steps to Retiring When You Want

Are you on track with being able to retire when you want to? It's so easy to procrastinate about investing money for your retirement – especially if you're a long ways away from your retirement date. But starting early makes it so much easier to meet your retirement goals.

How much do want to save? A million dollars? Keep in mind that no one reached age 65 and complained that they saved too much! Many folks believe that you have to have a significant income to save a million dollars, but nothing could be further from the truth.

Saving steadily and starting as soon as possible can make it possible for anyone to retire a millionaire.

Follow these steps to get yourself quickly on track:

1. **Take an assessment.** Where are you right now financially? How much have you saved so far? What is your current income? What are you current expenses? How much are you currently saving? What changes can you make right now that will make the biggest difference? Do you need the advice of an expert?

   - Your best plans for moving forward toward your goals begin with an accurate idea of where you are right now. Ascertain your progress at least every year.

2. **Start saving today.** Most of us would rather buy a new TV today than save for a retirement that might not happen for 30 years. If you can enroll in a program that has automatic deductions, like a company 401(k) plan or an automatic-deduction brokerage account, saving can be a lot easier.

   - How you save isn't nearly as important as the saving itself. Just start immediately! Even a relatively small amount can really add up over the years.

3. **Make a plan.** Make an honest evaluation of how much money you'll most likely need to retire and live comfortably for the remainder of your life. Then take a look at how much you need to save between now and then to make it happen. There are many financial planning calculators available online to help with your planning.

   - Imagine how much better your retirement savings would be right now if you had developed a plan and implemented it 10 years ago. Don't wait another day. Today is the day.

4. *The Power of Compounding.* In making your plan, remember the tremendous power of compounding! At 10% interest, an 18 year old only needs to save $20 a week to amass a million dollars by age 65. A 30 year old: $67 a week. A 40 year old: $188 a week. The earlier you start, the less painful the saving process will be.

   - Include other money that goes into your plan as well. For example, if your employer matches 100% of your retirement plan contributions, you only need to put in half the required amount. If you'll have other income in retirement, like rental or social security income or money from a business or trust, include those in your figures.

5. **Consider These 3 Factors.** *The 3 most important factors to your success are the rate of return, the amount of money being saved, and time.* So invest well, invest a lot, and invest as soon as you can. Maximizing these three factors to the best of your ability is really the key to retiring in style and as soon as possible.

You don't have to be wealthy to retire a millionaire if you live below your means, save, and invest. The most important thing is to start saving immediately.

Even with a lower middle-class income, you can easily become a millionaire by maximizing the rate of return, amount saved, and time. Get aggressive with your savings plan and you'll retire in style.

7 Effective Strategies to Reduce Estate Taxes

Even if you're not wealthy, an estate plan can ensure that your assets pass on to those whom you want to receive them.

Estate taxes are imposed on the heir of an estate and include any real estate, stock, cash, or other assets transferred to heirs at the time of death. There are both federal estate taxes and, in some states, state estate taxes.

Wouldn't you rather see these items stay in your family instead of being eaten by Uncle Sam?

Laws can vary from state to state, so be sure to find the details that apply to your situation.

Use these tips to reduce your estate tax burden:

1. **Give the money to your children while you're still alive.** In 2023, you can give up to $17,000 per year to any of your children or grandchildren. If you're married, you and your spouse can each give a total of $34,000 per child each year. This can add up.

2. **Be charitable.** ***Charitable gifts and lifetime transfers are a way to reduce your estate taxes and get your money to the organizations that mean the most to you.***

    - There are several ways to gift money and assets to charitable groups. Not surprisingly, charities are well versed in gift giving and taxes. Their help is also free!

3. **Set up a trust.** An irrevocable life insurance trust permits the transfer of assets up to the value of the life insurance premium. The real benefit comes from the value of the policy. **Life insurance proceeds are normally free from taxes.** This is quite simple to set up, but a trust attorney can ensure that it's done properly.

4. **Transfer assets to your spouse.** Gifts given during your lifetime or left to your spouse in your will are not subject to income taxes.

    - However, your spouse will eventually have to pay taxes upon their death. But this extra time can be put to good use to further reduce the tax liability.

5. **Enjoy it.** Any money spent won't be part of your estate come tax-time. If you've focused on saving in the past, maybe it's time to enjoy some of your money.

6. **Move.** *Not all states collect an estate or inheritance tax.* Moving to a different state could save your estate a lot of money. A little over half the states don't collect these taxes, and one of them may appeal to you. Do some calculations and see how much you would save if you moved.

7. **Set up a family partnership or family LLC.** These business entities are another way to potentially reduce estate taxes.

Estate planning isn't just about protecting your assets. It's also about meeting your financial goals. *If you don't have an estate plan, it's never too soon to start.* An attorney is a great place to begin. Just be sure that they have expertise in estate planning. For example, most attorneys don't have the slightest idea how to set up a trust.

If you have significant assets, estate taxes can approach 40% of the value of your estate. It only makes sense to reduce this burden as much as possible. Your heirs will thank you.

A Quick Guide to Funeral Expenses

Most of us refrain from thinking about death at all. However, considering your funeral expenses is important to you and your loved ones. At some point, someone will have to pay that bill. It would be helpful to know how much it's likely to cost so you can plan to have the funds available for your final wishes.

The cost of a traditional funeral is almost $8,000 or more. Prices can vary dramatically, though, depending upon the choices that are made.

Check out this quick breakdown of the costs:

- **Funeral home services: $1,500-$2,000**
    - This includes the filing of all the required permits and certificates, placing the obituary notice, making funeral arrangements with the cemetery, crematory, and caring for the remains until the burial.

- **Embalming: $750-$1,000**
    - This is not required by law but is necessary in certain cases.

- **Other preparations: $1,000-$2,000**
    - This can include such things as grooming and dressing the deceased, preparing the casket, bathing and disinfecting, refrigeration, and expedited cremation.

- **Transferring the remains to the funeral home: $350**
    - The funeral home must retrieve the remains from the hospital, nursing home, or other place of death.

- **Funeral home Facilities: $1,500-$2,000**
    - This cost primarily pays for the staff during the viewing.

- **Vehicles: $1,500-$2,000**
    - Included in this cost are the hearse and the vehicles that transport the flowers. Using the funeral homes vehicles to transport family members would be an additional cost.

- **Cremation: $700**
    - Cremation is less expensive than a casket and funeral plot.

- **Casket: $200-$10,000**
    - The quality and appearance of caskets can vary widely.

- **Cemetery plot: $400-$10,000**
    - It all depends on the cemetery you choose and where the plot is located. Location, location, location.

- **Other cemetery expenses: $1,000**
    - Most of this cost is related to placing the casket in the ground.

- **Grave marker: $500-$10,000**
    - Size, material, and complexity all contribute to the price.

Consider these costs and then make an appropriate plan for your funeral and buri-al. Let your loved ones know your plan. This will save your relatives from having to worry about it when that dreadful time comes.

Basic Investment Strategies

Understanding the Time Value of Money

You've probably heard that time is money and money is time. Well, it's true! In financial circles, there's something called the "time value of money." ***The time value of money is simply a concept to assign a worth to money based on different periods of time.***

For example, we can ask if you're better off having $1,000 today or $3,000 in twelve years. Which is more valuable? To be able to answer that question, you have to be able to calculate the future value of $1,000 over a twelve-year span.

Let's examine the concept of future value. We'll use our example of $1,000 now vs. $3,000 in 12 years. And let's assume that you expect to make 8% on your investments.

Figuring Future Value (FV):

Equation: $FV = \text{Original Amount} \times (1 + \text{interest rate})^{\text{time}}$

Plug in your numbers: $FV = \$1{,}000 \times (1 + 0.08)^{12}$

Calculate Answer: $FV = \$2{,}518.17$

This means that $3,000 in twelve years is more valuable because $1,000 now would only be worth $2,518.17 in twelve years.

Present Value

Just as money has a future value, it also has a present value. Using this concept, you can also solve the dilemma above by calculating the present value of the $3,000 that you'd receive twelve years in the future.

Present value looks at an amount of money to be received in the future and determines what it would be worth now.

Let's imagine you were going to receive $5,000 in five years. What would that be worth now? This is really just the reverse of finding the future value. Let's use an interest rate of 7%.

Figuring Present Value (PV)

Equation: PV = FV / (1+interest rate)^{time}

Plug in Your Numbers: PV = $5,000 / (1+0.07)^5

Calculate Answer: PV = $3,564.93

This means that $3,564.93 today would have the same value as $5,000 earned in five years.

Don't let these equations intimidate you. Calculators and spreadsheets make them a snap. Financial math is often quite simple, even if the exponents look daunting.

Now that you have these equations at hand, let's see what they can do for you personally. To start with, you could calculate what your investments will be worth in a certain number of years. You could also figure out what your savings account would be worth 20 years from now.

Let's suppose you wanted to have a million dollars in the bank in 25 years. You'd want to calculate how much money you would need now to make that happen in the given period of time. You could also look at the amount of money required to make a million dollars sooner than that.

Here are some of the most common situations where these calculations would be useful:

- Student loans
- Savings accounts
- Credit cards
- Mortgage payments
- Retirement planning
- Investments

Retirement planning is probably the most common activity for using these concepts. Try playing with a few examples from your own life. Figure out how much your 401k would be worth in the future if you never deposited another dime in the account. Investigate the future value of all your retirement investments.

However you go about using these equations, *now you can calculate exactly what time is really worth to you, in terms of money.* By utilizing the concepts of future value and present value, you'll never need to be confused again when you're comparing financial options. Dig into the math and apply it to you own life. There's no better way to learn.

Why Do Companies Care About Their Stock Prices?

It doesn't make a lot of sense to the casual observer why a company would be concerned about its stock price. After all, unless the company is currently issuing stock, it would appear that the stock price would be irrelevant to the company.

Consider that when you buy or sell stock, you're usually conducting transactions with other investors. So why would the company care about the price? ***It would seem that the rise or fall in a company's stock price would be inconsequential.***

The fact is, however, that the company cares a tremendous amount!

Let's take a look at some of the reasons for this:

1. **The shareholders care.** You'll commonly hear CEOs of public companies claim that their primary responsibility is to increase shareholder value.

    - ***At the end of the day, the CEO and the board of directors don't want to make the shareholders unhappy.***

    - When the shareholders are losing money, they can try to make changes in the current management because they do get to vote on things. In many cases, they can vote to send the executives packing.

2. **Prevent hostile takeover.** While private companies can only be bought out if the owners choose to sell, public companies can be taken over if enough of the stock is owned by a single investor or group of investors. When companies are taken over, the top-level people tend to lose their jobs, and no one likes to lose their job.

    - *Companies with a slumping stock price can be attractive takeover targets.* By keeping the stock price high, the assets of the company are more expensive for corporate raiders.

    - On the other hand, if the stock price is high, it also makes it easier for that company to take over other companies. This is usually accomplished by issuing additional shares.

3. **Borrowing money is cheaper.** *The stock price of a company is often used to gauge the financial health of the company.* If the stock price has been dropping, analysts and creditors tend to be more wary of that company's future profitability.

    - Over time, a company's earnings and stock price tend to be well correlated. A company with strong earnings is more likely to pay its debt obligations. As a result, with a strong stock price, the company is likely to get a better interest rate for loans.

    - A strong stock price also makes it more advantageous if the company wants to issue additional stock. They can raise the same amount of money by selling fewer shares than if the stock price were lower. The current shares are not diluted as much, and the damage to current stockholders is minimized.

4. **The executives are stockholders.** Typically, the executives in a public company hold a significant amount of stock and receive stock options. Those executives make a lot more money if the stock price is high. The founder of the company usually owns a lot of stock.

5. **Pride/ego:** All executives are aware of their next potential job. If they want to have the best opportunity to get ahead, they have to do a good job, and ***doing a good job is largely dependent on raising the stock price.*** Everyone wants to be viewed in a positive light.

Companies have several reasons to be concerned about their company's stock prices. Some of the reasons are self-serving, but it is in the shareholders' best interests that the stock price does well. The management, company, and shareholders are all threatened when the stock price falls.

What *Deal or No Deal* Can Teach You About Financial Risk Management

Who would have thought that you could learn about financial risk management from watching a television game show? That's right! ***Watching Deal or No Deal can actually help you make better investment decisions.***

If you've ever watched the show, you'll know that it's about attempting to analyze the results of risk taking. There are numbered briefcases, each with a hidden dollar value. Each case you pick earns you the dollar value hidden inside.

In its simplest form, it's a random system. But you've probably thought that you could figure out a pattern, right? Well, while you may have had some luck before, here are some key lessons that you can take away from the game.

1. **Random systems aren't predictable. *Simply put, avoid using past activities in a random system to predict future movement.*** When you're trying to decide which stock to buy, it's almost useless looking at its past performance.

    - An investment opportunity yielding a particular result in the past doesn't make it predisposed to produce in the same way again.

    - Avoid being deluded into thinking that you can see patterns of growth from past performance.

2. **Panic clouds judgment.** Have you made an investment that's now giving you negative results? Have you played the stock market only to realize that it's now on the decline? If you answered yes to either question, you've likely panicked at one point or another.

    - ***The first lesson to learn is panic almost always clouds judgment.*** The minute you realize your investment is going sour, you lose your composure. Try to avoid this.

    - With pending stock market declines, you may feel like you're at a crossroads. You may want to get out because you don't want to regret staying in. But allow yourself time to think it through. Determine which action can produce a result you can live with.

3. **Fear of loss drives decision-making.** ***The reality is that fear of loss is what pushes you to make a hasty decision.*** At least that's usually the case with questionable investments.

    - Because you fear what you might end up losing, you may end up opting out of your investment too soon. That may not be the best move. This is often the case with contestants on *Deal or No Deal*.

    - Giving thought to what you've lost up to this point can make you feel you took too long to sell. But be fair to yourself. ***Risky investments are largely based on probability.***

4. **Dwindling options promote risk-taking.** What the game show also shows is that as options dwindle, contestants become more risk-prone. ***Similarly, you could also be dwelling on past "losses" and that could affect rational assessment.***

    - Try to leave former investment experiences in the past. The same goes for past performance of current investments. Look at the current investment at face value.

    - Determine if you'll really be better off remaining in the game or pulling out with what you currently have.

So is *Deal or No Deal* just a game, or is it something that provides you with real lessons in financial risk-taking? It's definitely a little bit of both. ***You learn a little from every experience!***

Of course, it wouldn't be a wise idea to use this game show as your guide to financial wellness! But there's definitely no harm in using some of the examples to help in your decision-making. Learn these lessons, but seek the wisdom of the experts in your financial dealings as well.

Types of Mutual Funds

Trying to figure out which mutual fund to purchase can be a challenge! There are so many different types; where does one even start? We're going to look at the different types of mutual funds, which really is the first step to finding a fund that fits your needs.

At the most basic level, there are 4 main types of funds:

1. Equity Funds (Stocks)

- These funds that invest in company stocks are by far the largest category of funds. The objective of these funds tends to be centered on long-term growth with some income generation. There are numerous types of equity funds because there are many types of stocks. Some of the different classifications would include:
    - Global: Invest around the world, which could include your own country
    - International: Invest in countries outside of your own
    - Large-Cap: Companies with over $10 billion worth of total stock value
    - Mid-Cap: Companies between $2 billion and $10 billion worth of total stock value
    - Small-Cap: Companies with less than $2 billion worth of total stock value
    - Sector Funds: Target certain markets, such as technology, health, financial, and more
    - Index Funds: Seek to mirror a specific index, such as the NASDAQ or the NYSE

2. Fixed Income Funds (Bonds)

- These funds focus on purchasing government and corporate debt. While this sounds very simple, there are a wide variety of bond funds, the main differences being the amount of risk associated with the bonds being purchased.

- So a bond fund that invests in junk bonds is going to have a much higher level of risk than a fund that invests primarily in government bonds. But if everything goes according to plan, the junk bond fund should provide a much higher return.

3. Money Market Funds

- These funds only invest in short-term debt, like Treasury bills. The rate of return is better than your typical savings account, but not by much. These funds are typically used as an alternative to a conventional savings account.

4. Balanced Funds

- Balanced funds invest in both stocks and debt instruments. Again, there are a wide variety of funds, depending on the types of equities and the types of debt it purchases.

Now that you know the basics, it will make your challenge of choosing a mutual fund much easier. Keep increasing your investment IQ; after all, it's your money.

The Tax Advantages of Investing in ETFs

Exchange-Traded Funds (ETFs) have been available since 1993. They have grown in popularity every year since their inception. *A simple way to view ETFs is to consider them mutual funds that trade like stocks.*

Remember, mutual fund shares are always purchased and sold directly. The tax advantages are one of the most significant advantages of ETFs.

Consider these differences between how mutual funds and exchange-traded funds are taxed:

1. **Mutual fund gains are not tax-deferred.** Because an active fund manager trades the assets of a mutual fund, capital gains taxes must be paid whenever equities are sold for a profit. *Over time, these taxes can significantly erode your gains.*

2. **Mutual fund investors incur capital gains taxes via 3 events:**

   - Shareholder redemption can trigger a tax event. If the monetary amount of shareholders leaving the fund is greater than the amount of shareholder joining the fund, a sale of the funds equities will most likely occur.

   - Portfolio turnover can also trigger capital gains taxes when equity is sold for a profit.

   - Corporate actions are the third tax-triggering event. Stock splits, acquisitions, and similar activities can also trigger a tax event, depending on the details of the corporate action.

3. **The creation and redemption processes are different:**

    - The mutual fund creates new shares by using the investor's money to purchase the proper amount of shares of stock or an appropriate amount of bonds. When the investor sells their mutual fund shares, the fund must sell equities to raise the money to return the same value of those shares to the investor.

    - An investor in an ETF simply buys the shares from another investor on the exchange that lists the ETF. This means no new shares are created. ***When the investor wants to cash out, he simply sells his shares to another investor via the same process.***

4. **ETF capital gains taxes exist but are incurred differently.** The capital gains tax only becomes due when you sell your stake in the ETF. ***Taxes are never due while you are still holding the ETF.***

    - ETFs do not turn over their assets at a high rate, but some turnover does occur. The taxes on these gains are not realized until the entire stake in the ETF has been sold to another investor. Therefore, all your realized gains continue to grow. This is significantly different from having to pay those taxes each year, which is limiting.

    - Mutual funds must sell equities whenever someone wishes to sell their shares. Since an ETF is traded like a stock, investor turnover has little effect on the asset turnovers in an ETF.

    - This in-kind redemption process permits the ETF manager to sell the lower cost-basis stocks through transfers, minimizing or avoiding taxes. These in-kind transactions aren't considered sales, so no tax is triggered.

- There is greater tax efficiency with an ETF since the activity of the shareholders and the subsequent equities transactions have a minimal effect on the portfolio.

- ***The after-tax returns are usually quite better with an ETF than a mutual fund that tracks a similar index.***

ETFs offer many of the advantages of mutual funds but usually have less tax exposure. Many investors underestimate the impact of taxes on their long-term success.

Deferring taxes is highly advantageous, because you can continue to earn money on the capital you would have turned over to the government in the form of taxes. It could be very beneficial for you to take a serious look at exchange-transfer funds.

7 Ways to Reduce Taxes on Mutual Fund Investments

Mutual funds can be a great way to invest because they have many advantages. ***However, mutual funds also have a lot of tax complications.*** Most investors aren't aware of the associated tax issues when they first invest in mutual funds, but they're important concerns.

If taxes are having a significant impact on your mutual fund returns, there are steps you can take to address tax issues.

Here are 7 ways to reduce taxes on your mutual fund investments:

1. **Avoid purchasing shares before an ex-dividend distribution.** Funds pay their capital gains distributions on a specific date.

    - It doesn't matter whether you owned the shares for 1 day or 10 years, you're immediately going to be responsible for tax on the capital gains. This is true even you didn't own shares in the fund when the gain was realized.

    - Check and see when the fund makes its distributions. If it is happening soon, just wait until the date has passed.

    - Most distributions happen towards the end of the calendar year. That is why ***the beginning of the year is a great time to purchase mutual funds.***

2. **Put your high-yield funds in tax-deferred accounts.** All other things being equal, high-yield means high-tax. If possible, own these investments in tax-deferred accounts where the tax penalty will be minimized and your long-term gains will be the greatest.

3. **Take a look at Exchange Traded Funds (ETFs) instead of mutual funds.** ETFs usually have a lower tax consequence than actively managed mutual funds.

    - These portfolios tend to be more stable since ETFs managers don't have to sell securities to make capital gains distributions.

4. **Consider funds that are more tax efficient.** *There are mutual funds that are managed with the intention of minimizing the tax burden incurred by the investor.*

    - This is accomplished via municipal bonds, avoiding regular bonds, and utilizing any losses to offset any gains.
    - Funds that specialize in municipal bonds can potentially avoid both state and federal taxes.

5. **Choose a fund with a lower level of turnover.** Funds that churn through many investments can create a tax burden on the investor, even if the fund's share price drops.

    - It is almost always true that a fund with fewer turnovers in its investments will result in less tax burden and is also a sign that a fund has a long-term approach to investing.

6. **Take full advantage of IRA, 401(k), and other tax-deferred investment accounts.** Your investments will grow at a much greater rate if you can refrain from pulling money out of them to pay taxes. True, you will have to pay the tax someday, but your nest egg will grow much larger in these accounts.

7. **Plan ahead.** Anytime you consider selling shares in a fund, consider the tax implication. It would be best if you have the resources available to pay the taxes without having to dip into other investments.

- Make certain you have the money set-aside and available when tax time arrives.

- Remember that investments held for a minimum of a year are taxed at a lower rate than investments held for less than a year.

There are many ways to minimize the taxes realized with mutual fund ownership. However, taxes are not the only consideration.

Sometimes it is best to sell and lock in your profits rather than hold on to an investment for tax purposes. Always let common sense be your guide.

6 Ways to Invest in Gold

There is something exciting and exotic about owning gold. Gold has been a standard form of currency for a very long time. *Gold can provide protection against inflation and many financial advisors recommend owning some gold in your portfolio.*

There are several options for being invested in gold; some of them are direct, like owning gold bars. Others are indirect, like owning stock in a gold mine.

Let's look at your options:

1. **Exchange Traded Funds:** *This is the easiest way to own gold, since you don't have to store or insure it.* One share of an ETF is equivalent to a specific amount of gold, frequently a fraction of an ounce. These shares can be bought and sold just like any other mutual fund share or share of stock.

    - The annual expense of owning these shares is quite low; usually less than 0.5% annually; this is better than the expense ratio of most mutual funds.

2. **Mutual Funds:** There are many mutual funds that own gold in some form, but there are relatively few that invest in gold exclusively. Most of these funds invest vertically in gold related businesses. This means they invest in gold bullion, the mines and other related real estate, the mining companies, distribution, and more.

3. **Futures and Options:** These provide a vehicle to bet on the future price of gold. You can purchase the right to buy or sell gold at a predetermined price within a predetermined span of time into the future. *This type of investing in gold can carry a high risk and involve complex techniques, so be sure to research strategies before you commit.*

4. **Gold Mining Companies:** Many gold mining companies issue stock just like other publicly traded companies. These can be found on the various stock exchanges. As with any stock, doing your homework on the company you're investing in is critical.

    - Keep in mind that there is always a surplus of gold in the world; the actual commercial demand is very low relative the supply. ***The value of gold is almost entirely dependent on investor sentiment.***

5. **Jewellery:** This is a very difficult way to invest in gold, as the value of the jewelry is often much greater than the underlying value of the gold in the jewelry. In general, the only person making money on gold jewelry is the jewelry shop owner.

6. **Gold Bullion:** While most people think of gold bars, the term 'gold bullion' applies to any pure or nearly pure gold with a certified weight and purity. Smaller bars and coins are more practical for most people. One large gold bar worth $250,000 isn't easy to chop in pieces if you need some of that money now.

    - Gold coins and smaller bars can be purchased from dealers for a 1-3% premium over the value of the gold they contain. The values of coins are easy to determine in the financial marketplace and dealers are easy to find in decent sized cities.
    - However, insurance and storage costs could use up part of your investment funds, so it's a good idea to consider these fees when looking at the feasibility of investing in gold coins.
    - Common gold coins include the South African Krugerrand, the Canadian maple leaf, and the U.S. eagle coins.

There are many options to invest in gold. Bullion can make sense for larger investors with the ability to store and insure that gold. The average person that wants exposure to the price of gold would be better served by owning shares in an ETF or gold-related mutual fund.

Those with an aggressive stream can look into options and futures. Owning stock in gold companies themselves is another option if you have the time to do the research.

Each of these options could work for you, depending on your situation. If you want to invest in gold, your best option is really to choose the vehicle that works best for your investment needs.

8 Ways to Invest in Foreign Markets

The United States might have the largest economy in the world, but it's far from the *only* economy. **There's a whole world out there.** When the US economy is faltering, there are plenty of other economies doing well. It's much easier to invest successfully in a thriving economy than in one that's struggling.

But most investors don't know where to start. Do you get on the phone and call Tokyo when you want to invest in a Japanese stock?

In 2012, the US was less than 19% of the world economy. In 2021, the US's share was 13.6%. This means the overall That's a lot for one country, but it's still a small amount compared to the combined rest of the world. Do you think there might a few good investments in that other 86%? Of course!

Fortunately, there are several easy ways to invest overseas:

1. **American Depository Receipts (ADR).** These are US traded stocks that represent foreign stocks. If you've ever owned Sony stock, you almost certainly owned ADR shares. You didn't actually own a share of actual Sony stock.

    - These are traded on the US stock exchanges and are quoted in US dollars. This eliminates the need for currency conversions.

2. **Buy the stock on a foreign exchange.** Not all foreign stocks can be purchased with ADRs. ***Many foreign stocks can be purchased on the London or Toronto stock exchanges.*** There are international brokerage houses that can help with this type of investment, but the fees can be steep. Check before you buy.

3. **International Mutual Funds.** There are US funds that invest exclusively in foreign markets. International funds tend to invest with a broad scope.

4. **Regional Mutual Funds.** These are similar to international funds, but tend to invest within a certain region, such as the Middle East.

5. **Country Mutual Funds.** These are limited to a specific country, such as China or Russia.

6. **Sector Funds.** *Sector Funds stay within an industry, but cross borders.* A sector fund that invests in gold mining all over the world would be an example.

7. **Exchange Traded Fund (ETF).** An ETF is like a mutual fund that tracks a specific index. For example, there is an Oil Index (OSX) that is composed of 15 different stocks. An ETF mimics an index. Many ETFs contain foreign stocks. This is a great way to invest internationally within an industry.

    - *ETFs are priced, purchased, and sold like stocks.* Remember that mutual funds are priced at the net asset value (NAV). The price of an ETF is whatever the market will bear. Mutual fund shares are always sold at their actual value. Still, it wouldn't be a bad idea to try pricing an ETF with the NAV and see where it stands.

8. **Invest in foreign currency.** Currency trading can be exciting and serves as an excellent means to reduce risk in foreign investments.

    - However, currency trading is not for the weak of heart. Many people have made a fortune in currency trading. Many have been wiped out. If you have the expertise, it can be a great way to invest in a foreign market.

There are several ways to invest in foreign markets. It's time that investors opened their eyes to all the investing opportunities around the world. There are many companies and investment vehicles based in other countries. ***It would be a shame to miss out on all these foreign economies.***

The US is less than 15% of the global economy. If you're not investing internationally, you're missing out on over 85% of the opportunity! Look abroad for your next investment for fun and profits.

Growth Investing Made Simple

Are you a newly retired baby boomer looking to make the most out of your current savings? Perhaps you're younger and looking for a way to increase your investment earnings at a faster rate.

Growth investing is fast becoming a popular investment choice for those seeking to achieve higher returns on their investments in less time.

Investing for growth is set apart from other investing strategies due to one major difference. Most investment strategies involve monitoring the historic trends of a stock while juxtaposing this information with a stock's current performance in order to help determine the possibility of future growth.

If you're investing specifically for growth, however, you'll focus more on current factors and will often have less historical information to base your investment decisions on.

If you think there's increased risk to this investment strategy, you're correct. However, there are also benefits that accompany the risks.

By being the first to invest in a high-potential stock, you'll reap greater rewards than those who follow afterwards. This is the main principle of growth investing at work and makes this a highly lucrative way to invest your money.

Let's look at some of the other key components involved in investing for growth.

Probability

Make probability your friend. If you have little historical information to base your investment decision on, you'll want to use sound mathematics and probability to weigh the profitability of your stock picks.

- ***Probability*** is the chance that your stock will perform favorably and give you a return on your investment

- ***Magnitude*** is the amount of earnings you expect to reap if your stock performs favorably.

- ***Expected Return*** is the final calculation that takes into account how much you stand to gain when your stock performs favorably and how much you stand to lose if it performs poorly.

If you're still not sure how all of these terms relate to making a sound investment decision, the following question sums up the entire principle quite nicely:

How much money will I make if I'm right and how much will I lose if I'm wrong?

If you stand to gain a lot when you're right and lose very little when wrong, this is an ideal investment scenario if you're investing for growth.

Common Sense

It may be a challenge to predict which forms of technology will become big in the future. Who could have predicted that cell phones would be as popular as they are now when they were still in the early stages of development? How about bottled water? If you predicted these immensely popular trends, then you might be reading this article from your yacht in Monaco.

While it may be difficult to predict the future, you can use what you already know to help you make sound investment decisions.

What do you already know? Probably more than you think.

Take typewriters, for example. Investing in a technology that is obviously outdated and becoming closer to extinction is not a profitable move to make. There are many types of investments for which you can use your common sense in order to determine if the overall forecast seems favorable or not.

Economic Trends

Follow a top-down macroeconomic model. Rather than worrying about what other investors are saying is a "hot pick," look at the larger economic picture.

- Look at what's happening in the economy. Is there a large-scale trend happening in any major industry?
- Consider what sectors will benefit from these trends and other changes that are taking place in the economy.
- Look at companies that are in those sectors that are best able to deliver to the market what it needs.

Investing for growth uses large-scale trends to help make investment decisions. Start thinking about what you hear or read in the news each day. ***Ask yourself what areas of the economy are changing and what new types of needs are emerging?*** These questions will help point you towards potential stocks that are conducive to growth investing.

Investing in Foreign Stocks

At some point, every investor wonders if he should invest in foreign companies. It's not uncommon to hear about the great profits that can be made, though those profits can come at additional risk.

Stocks in the United States only account for about 15% of the total value of the stock in the world. So, more than 85% of the stock value is outside our borders. That's hard to ignore if you're a serious investor.

In fact, many of the largest companies in the world, especially those that make electronics, steel, and perform mining are outside the United States. There are over a dozen significant stock markets based in other countries. More importantly, many of these companies operate in economies that are growing very rapidly.

Wouldn't it be nice to always be investing in economies that are moving in a positive direction?

Foreign companies are a good way to diversify. They also lack correlation with the US markets. What does that mean? It means they don't go up and down together, so when the US markets are down, it's likely to be up somewhere else. Of course that doesn't mean they're always opposite each other.

The United States has significant economic impact on the rest of the world, but ***research shows the foreign markets are independent enough that they can help even out your portfolio over time.***

Risk

There is additional risk with investing in foreign markets:

1. **Currency risk.** If the currency of your foreign company goes down in value relative to the US dollar, you're likely to lose money. But you're more likely to make money if it goes up.

2. **Country risk.** Country risk can include these important factors and more:

    - Many countries have unstable political climates.
    - Some are very prone to getting earthquakes and typhoons.
    - The country may be unstable economically.

Evaluation

Do you think it's tough to evaluate a company in the USA? In many foreign countries, businesses aren't as regulated and aren't required to provide the same information to investors as companies here. Even worse than no information is inaccurate information; ***the quality of the information you're given is likely to be of questionable validity.***

It's also important to consider the tax implications. Every country has different laws; some won't tax you at all, while others might impose very high taxes and fees on your investments. It's really a function of how interested they are in having foreign investors. So in doing your research on the companies involved in your investment, also look into the tax consequences.

ADRs

If you're hesitant to dive in and buy stocks on the foreign markets, there is an alternative, though it can be somewhat limited. ***American depository receipts (ADRs) are a way to buy shares in foreign companies on the US stock exchanges.*** These companies generally comply with the US reporting laws and regulations, so the information you get may be more accurate.

With ADRs, you'll typically be limited to the larger and more well-known companies. For example, if you buy Sony stock in the United States, you are buying ADRs.

US Multinationals

Also consider that you can get some international exposure by purchasing shares of US companies with large overseas operations. Coca-Cola is a good example; over half of their revenue is from foreign operations.

Diversification

Investing in foreign stocks can be a great way to diversify your portfolio. ***The rewards can be great, but you'll have to put in a little extra time to get the information you need to make wise decisions.***

It won't be long before you'll be telling your neighbors about your holdings in Russia and Brazil. Do your research and then diversify with foreign stocks!

Mid-Cap Stocks for Beginners

Mid-cap stocks are categorized as those companies with a market capitalization between $2 billion and $10 billion. Usually, they're well-established companies somewhere between the slower growing large-caps and the rapidly growing small-caps. ***Recently, mid-cap stocks have done better than both the large-cap and small-cap competition with very little added risk.***

We're going to examine the principal characteristics of mid-cap stocks as well as how to analyze them and why you should strongly consider these often-ignored investments for your portfolio.

Why They Should be Part of Your Portfolio

The better historical performance isn't the only reason you might want to consider mid-caps as part of your portfolio. Several additional characteristics are valuable as well:

- The majority of mid-caps are simply small-caps that grew bigger over time. Additional growth will give them the opportunity to eventually become large-cap businesses.

- Part of expanding is the ability to obtain additional financing to support that growth. This is much more difficult for small-cap companies to do.

- ***The principal advantage over large-caps relates to earnings growth.*** Mid-cap companies haven't yet reached the stage where earnings diminish and dividends have become a significant part of a stock's total return.

- Maybe the most overlooked reason for investing money in mid-caps is that they get less analyst coverage than the large-caps. **Many of the greatest performing stocks have been ignored businesses that suddenly became popular,** generating the institutional purchasers that are essential to push their price higher.

In the end, investing in mid-caps makes sense because they provide investors the best of both worlds: small-cap growth along with large-cap stability.

Profitability

One of the great things about mid-cap stocks is that the businesses are generally profitable and have been for quite awhile.

Consider these advantages:

- Mid-cap companies usually have experienced management teams.

- On the average, a mid-cap's earnings tend to grow at a quicker rate than the average small-cap and accomplish this with less volatility and risk.

- Along with earnings growth, the mid-cap company is in a good position to maintain their earnings for the foreseeable future. That's what ultimately turns a mid-cap into a large-cap.

- Clues that suggest a corporation's earnings are headed in the right direction include growing gross and operating margins in combination with lower inventories and accounts receivable. Turning inventory and receivables faster usually leads to greater cash flow and increased profits.

All of these features also help reduce risk. Mid-caps tend to have these attributes more frequently than small or large-caps.

Growth

Revenue and earnings growth are two of the most important factors to long-term returns.

Recently, mid-cap stocks have done better than both large-cap and small-cap stocks due to their higher growth in both revenue and earnings. It's likely that the ability of mid-caps to respond faster than large-caps, and their greater financial stability compared to small-caps, are their greatest advantages.

When researching a mid-cap firm, look into the quality of their revenue growth:

- When gross margins, operating margins, and revenues are all increasing, it's an excellent indicator that the company is developing greater economies of scale, resulting in higher shareholder profits.

- Another great indicator of healthy revenue growth is when lowered total debt improves cash flow.

Consider adding mid-cap stocks to your portfolio. There's a lot to like about them. ***The great opportunities for both profitability and growth, along with the relatively low risk, can make them an excellent addition.*** Do some research and find a couple of good mid-caps; you'll be glad you did.

Stock Indexes Around the World

If you have an interest in what's going on in the world's financial markets, you can get familiar with these stock indexes from all over the world. Who knows, your next investment might be in Australia, Europe or Asia!

If you like to invest in mutual funds, there are index funds for just about any stock index. These funds spread out your risk over all the stocks in the index and mimic the performance of the index as a whole.

Country	Stock Index	Website
Australia	Australia ASX All Ordinaries	
Brazil	Brazil Bovespa Stock Index	http://www.bmfbovespa.com.br/en-us/home.aspx
Canada	Canada S&P/TSX 60	http://www.standardandpoors.com/indices/sp-tsx-60/en/us/?indexId=spcadntx--caduf--p-ca-l--
Chile	Santiago Index IPSA	http://www.bolsadesantiago.com/index.aspx
China	Shanghai Composite	http://www.sse.com.cn/sseportal/en_us/ps/home.shtml
Europe	Euronext 100	http://www.euronext.com/trader/summarizedmarket/stocks-2634-EN-FR0003502079.html?selectedMep=1
France	CAC 40	http://www.euronext.com/trader/summarizedmarket/stocks-2634-EN-FR0003500008.html?selectedMep=1

Country	Index	URL
Germany	DAX	http://deutsche-boerse.com/dbag/dispatch/en/kir/gdb_navigation/home
Hong Kong	Hang Seng	http://www.hsi.com.hk/
India	Mumbai Sensex	http://www.bseindia.com/
Japan	Nikkei	http://e.nikkei.com
Mexico	Mexican Bolsa	http://www.bmv.com.mx/
Switzerland	Swiss Market Index	http://www.six-swiss-exchange.com/indices/shares/smi_family_en.html
Taiwan	Taiwan TSEC 50 Index	http://www.twse.com.tw/en/
United Kingdom	FTSE 100	http://www.ftse.com/Indices/UK_Indices/index.jsp
United States	Dow Jones Industrial Average	http://www.djaverages.com/index.cfm?go=industrial-overview
United States	S&P 500 Index	http://www.standardandpoors.com/indices/sp-500/en/us/?indexId=spusa-500-usduf--p-us-l--

For true diversity in your investment portfolio, consider investing in other countries. This listing of stock indexes will help you get started today!

The Basics of Value Investing

Value investing is a school of thought regarding the selection of investments. ***Ben Graham and David Dodd, from the Columbia School of Business, started teaching the idea of value investing in 1928.*** Experts define value investing in many ways and have many conflicting opinions about it. But, most theories include finding underpriced investments via fundamental analysis.

Warren Buffett was a pupil of Graham's. While Graham was likely to purchase nearly any stock that met certain fundamental analysis metrics, Buffett didn't stop there. He was more concerned about the future prospects of a business. Graham didn't recommend using future projections, since they were unknown values.

Mr. Buffet uses a fundamental analysis to ensure a company is financially solid and likely to weather difficult financial times. He also looks for undervalued companies.

Academics have studied the viability of value stock picking strategies and have found them to be superior to both the growth strategies and the market overall. However, this advantage is only found in the long-term.

Check out these key points regarding value investing:

1. **Value investing largely consists of focusing on companies that are selling at a discount compared to the intrinsic value.** ***The intrinsic value can be thought of as the true value of a company's stock.*** It isn't just the assets.

It also includes intangible factors.

- A value investor is seeking a stock that's being undervalued by the market. The actual intrinsic value can't be truly determined with absolute certainty.

- If a company has a certain amount of physical inventory in the form of construction materials, a valuation is accurate. However, intrinsic value is more challenging to determine in more technological companies. Companies with intellectual assets are especially difficult to value accurately.

2. **The intrinsic value of a business is much greater than the sum of its assets.** For example, Coca-Cola is much more valuable than its buildings and beverage concentrate inventory. The brand, customer loyalty, and expected future earnings make it much more valuable.

    - However, when a business completely fails, the intrinsic value may be very close to the market value of the underlying assets.
    - *Though quite rare, it's possible to find companies whose assets alone exceed their stock valuation.*

3. **Many websites and brokerage firms assign values to stocks that are meant to represent the intrinsic value.** This might be a good starting point to start your own research.

    - ***Predicting future earnings, dividends, and other metrics 10 years into the future isn't an exact science.***

4. **The spread between the intrinsic value and the current price is commonly referred to as the "margin of safety."** So a stock selling at $60 per share, but valued by you to be worth $80 per share, has a 25% margin of safety since $60 is 25% less than $80.

5. **Value investing requires a significant time horizon.** If the market has undervalued a company, it can take many years for the reality to catch up to the illusion.

Value investing is a great methodology for those willing to put in the necessary time and effort to accurately value companies. ***Investing requires great patience and the avoidance of emotional decision-making.*** Logic and rational thinking are critical components to one's success.

If you've been investing without doing extensive research, it might be worth considering a more analytical approach. The numbers aren't the entire story, but they're certainly a significant factor.

What is Bitcoin and Cryptocurrency?

A cryptocurrency is a form of currency that has become popular over the last several years. Cryptocurrency is created by using the encryption techniques of computing and mathematics.

These techniques allow us to transfer funds and verify that the transfer did, in fact, occur. Another essential aspect of cryptocurrency is that it is independent of governments and central banks, making them decentralized.

These days, many important banks are becoming increasingly involved with the same kind of technology that underlies cryptocurrency. However, it is essential to understand that any currency that arises from their endeavors won't be true cryptocurrency because it will be controlled by the banks. The most reliable and most dedicated advocates of cryptocurrency are determined that it will not be centralized.

How Did Cryptocurrencies Develop?

Bitcoin is the most well-known cryptocurrency on the market. It has been the recipient of hype, fame, and publicity. The general public has been fascinated by its extraordinary increase in value over the last several years. They have been awestruck by the tales of significant wealth that has been generated with bitcoin, for those who acquired it in its infancy, when it was cheap.

Despite its novelty, people quickly realize that bitcoin is genuine money. In addition to bitcoin, there are many other cryptocurrencies, who like bitcoin, have had massive increases in their dollar value. Legitimate government and businesses are pursuing an increasing involvement in cryptocurrency. Despite critics, the market for these currencies is thriving.

Cryptocurrencies, Fiat Currencies, and Stocks

Fiat currencies are the currencies we use daily, like the dollar, yen, euro, and renminbi. Despite having the word currency in the word cryptocurrency, they are more similar to stocks and shares of the stock market than between fiat currencies and cryptocurrency.

When you purchase cryptocurrency, you get some of the coins for that cryptocurrency, which acts like a technology stock and a digital entry into a ledger, known as a blockchain.

Please Note: Since the purpose of this book is to focus on personal finance strategies, the author will not be going into detail about bitcoin, blockchain and investment strategies regarding cryptocurrencies. That is beyond the scope of this book.

However, if you would like to learn more about bitcoin, blockchain and in-depth strategies getting started, check out Andy's titles specifically on bitcoin, blockchain and cryptocurrency investing. These titles are available on Amazon:

- Step-By-Step Guide to Investing in Bitcoin: A Beginners Guide to Bitcoin, Digital Assets and CryptoCurrencies (Personal Finance Strategies for Every Stage of Life Series)

- Bitcoin Smart Kids – Teaching Kids of Every Age About Bitcoin
- Metaverse Smart Kids – Teaching Kids of Every Age About the Metaverse
- Blockchain Smart Kids - Teaching Kids of Every Age How the Blockchain and Bitcoin Work Together

How to Avoid These Common Bitcoin Mistakes

Over the past few decades, our lives have been transformed by the Internet. We now socialize online, get our news online, manage our money and buy everything we need online. Thanks to technology we no longer have to bother with the tedious tasks of remembering and thinking.

Unfortunately, this could lead to financial ruin when it comes to investing in bitcoin and blockchain technology. Here is a list of the most common Bitcoin mistakes and how you can avoid them.

Not Slowing Down

So many of us are used to sending and spending money online these days that we hardly think when we hand over our credit card to settle expenses. While this is fine when you are dealing with a credit card transaction that can be easily reversed, it's not the case with Bitcoin.

One of bitcoins features that make it unique is the fact that transactions are irreversible. This means that no matter how much you beg, once you send Bitcoin, it is never coming back. This is why you have to be extremely mindful every time you send or spend bitcoin.

Not Being Educated

Bitcoin and cryptocurrency are extremely hot right now. The problem with this is that the majority of the population doesn't fully understand cryptocurrency and the blockchain. One of the worst things that you can do when investing in Bitcoin is allowed your strategy to be guided by the media hype or by a fear of missing out. It will be far better if you take the time to educate yourself with at least the basics of bitcoin, blockchain, and cryptocurrency.

Panicking

As far as currencies go, cryptocurrency is a baby, and it still hasn't found its footing. You have to be prepared for this volatility before you even think about entering the market. If you don't then you will surely panic and buy when it's high and then panic sell when it's low and going down. Take the time to plan a long-term strategy rather than focusing on the daily changes in price.

Placing All Your Coins in One Basket

One of the most common mistakes made with buying, selling, and trading bitcoins is putting all your coins in one basket. If you are planning on investing heavily in bitcoin, you want to spread the coins out between several, adequately secured wallets. This way if one wallet gets hacked or lost, or you forget your password, you won't lose all your bitcoins.

History has a habit of repeating itself, but if you keep these common pitfalls in mind when you start investing in cryptocurrency, you'll be well ahead of the rest of the pack.

Deals of the Month

This section of the book is very unique. One vital aspect of personal finance is using your money to its fullest potential. This means getting the most value for your money.

In the "Deals of the Month" chapter, you'll learn the best time of the year to purchase certain items including groceries, cars, electronics and more. Many readers have shared their success stories of saving money by following the monthly suggestions in this chapter.

JANUARY

Deals of the Month:
January

Ring in the New Year by taking advantage of some great food sales in January. Plan to cook up some soups and stock up on diet foods.

Check out the groceries that will be a steal this month:

- ☐ Broccoli
- ☐ Cabbage
- ☐ Cauliflower
- ☐ Chocolate (holiday clearance)
- ☐ Diet foods
- ☐ Frozen hors d'hoeuvres
- ☐ Grapefruits
- ☐ Leeks
- ☐ Lemons
- ☐ Oatmeal
- ☐ Oranges
- ☐ Soda pop
- ☐ Tangelos
- ☐ Tangerines

Your local discount stores and home improvement stores will have the biggest sales in January on non-food items. They want to move all the left-over goods off their floors to make way for new items. Look for some whopping big savings on:

- ☐ Air conditioners
- ☐ Bicycles
- ☐ Cameras
- ☐ Carpeting and flooring
- ☐ Christmas decorations and gift wrap
- ☐ Electronics
- ☐ Exercise equipment
- ☐ Furniture
- ☐ Linens
- ☐ Small appliances
- ☐ Sneakers
- ☐ Televisions
- ☐ Toys
- ☐ Winter clothing

Looking for a new home, boat, or motorcycle? January is the month to buy those items at slashed costs. If you have some spare cash in the bank, think about the money you can save on the items you need this month.

Seek out the best buys to get the most bang for your buck in January!

Deals of the Month: February

Although grocery prices seem to keep going up and up, you can still find some genuine deals at the grocery store in February.

February is the month to stock up on canned foods:

- ☐ Beans
- ☐ Corn
- ☐ Tomatoes
- ☐ Soups

If you prefer fresh, go for cauliflower and broccoli. Fruits on the cheap will be grapefruit and oranges.

Valentine's Day will be long gone, but all the chocolate and candy won't. And it will be on sale for half-price or maybe even less.

You'll find oatmeal at rock-bottom prices, so buy a couple of extras.

Your best non-food deals in February will be on:

- ☐ Toothpaste
- ☐ Toothbrushes
- ☐ Mouthwash
- ☐ Tools

Visit your local discount and big box stores for these February bargains:

- Big screen TVs (after all, the Super Bowl will be televised in January or February)
- Boats
- Cameras
- Recliners

Enjoy your February by staying in and fixing plenty of hot soups while watching your new television or playing with your new camera. Before you know it, spring will arrive!

DEALS OF THE MONTH: March

MARCH

Before you know it, the first day of spring will be here. Along with March's arrival, grocery stores will offer some nice buys.

The National Frozen and Refrigerated Foods Association has declared March to be National Frozen Food Month. And who will benefit from this designation? You, the shopper!

You'll notice several coupons for frozen food items and great sales at your grocery store, too. Combine the two of them and you'll save big money. It's definitely the month to stock the freezer.

- ☐ Frozen Foods
- ☐ Lettuce
- ☐ Mangoes
- ☐ Pineapples

Non-food items are also available at bargain basement pricing. Boats are on sale again this month as showrooms need to be cleared for the new incoming models.

If you love good deals on perfume, March is your month. Because the perfume industry's biggest shopping days are in December (holidays) and February (Valentine's Day), their figures take a dive in March. So, in order to keep moving perfume off the shelves in March, they mark down their prices.

Also, it's almost time for gardening! Gardening tools are also on special this month, so check your wish list for garden implements.

If you don't mind last year's patterns, flatware and China will also be on sale in March. Here's the quick list of March non-food deals:

- ☐ Boats
- ☐ Perfumes
- ☐ Gardening Tools
- ☐ Flatware
- ☐ China
- ☐ Luggage

Fill your freezer with frozen food deals this month. Then, prepare for gardening by purchasing all the tools you need on sale. Finally, take advantage of pricing on perfumes. When it's all over, don't be surprised if you find yourself looking forward to next March!

Deals of the Month: April

APRIL

With several religious holidays this month, you'll likely be preparing some big meals.

Thankfully, there are also plenty of deals at the grocery store for ingredients you'll need to cook up those feasts. In April, you'll discover great buys on the following:

- Ham
- Eggs
- Candy (especially if you wait until after Easter)
- Rolls and prepared dough products
- Pre-made pie crusts
- Frozen pies
- Cake mixes and frosting
- Asparagus
- Broccoli
- Lettuce
- Mushrooms

You'll find some very good prices for non-food items as well. Whether you need some new sneakers, or want to cook your holiday dishes in new pots and pans, it's time to go shopping! Check out this list of April bargains:

- Athletic shoes
- Cookware
- Electronics
- Fabric
- Tires and other car accessories

Deals of the Month: May

Summer is upon us and soon, the kids will be out of school. And what do they like to eat? Picnic food! So, grocery-shopping this month is rewarding because the best kid-friendly and summer-fun foods are on special this month.

Check out these groceries available at slashed costs:

- ☐ Barbeque sauce
- ☐ Buns for hamburgers and hot dogs
- ☐ Chips
- ☐ Frozen pies
- ☐ Hotdogs
- ☐ Ground beef
- ☐ Ice cream
- ☐ Mushrooms
- ☐ Mustard
- ☐ Popsicles
- ☐ Relish
- ☐ Salad dressing
- ☐ Soda pop and bottled water

Stock up on early-ripening fruits and vegetables available on the cheap:

- ☐ Apricots
- ☐ Artichokes
- ☐ Broccoli
- ☐ Cherries
- ☐ Lettuce
- ☐ Pineapples
- ☐ Rhubarb
- ☐ Spring peas
- ☐ Zucchini

May is everyone's favorite time to get together for an impromptu backyard barbecue or picnic. Some of this month's non-food items on special will come in handy at your get-togethers:

- ☐ Disposable cups and plates
- ☐ Grill supplies—lighter fluid and charcoal
- ☐ Paper napkins and plastic utensils

Other low-priced goods in May include refrigerators, vacuums, cookware sets, and pet supplies.

Enjoy the weather and the savings this merry month of May!

JUNE

DEALS OF THE MONTH:
June

Summer gets into full swing this month. **Check out the June deals at your local grocery stores.**

Go ahead and buy some extras while they're on sale to save some money over the next few months as you partake in summer activities.

Here are some of the items that will be on sale in June:

- ☐ Bottled water
- ☐ Soda
- ☐ Tea bags
- ☐ Iced tea mixes
- ☐ Frozen treat novelties
- ☐ Ice cream

Looking for fresh produce? You'll also find deals on these delectable fruits and veggies:

- ☐ Cantaloupe
- ☐ Corn
- ☐ Blueberries
- ☐ Lettuce
- ☐ Peaches
- ☐ Strawberries
- ☐ Watermelon

On non-food items, you'll get some great buys on dishes in June. Later, around Father's Day, look for sales on tools for Dad.

As summer approaches, you might be thinking more and more about getting into shape. June is a great time to check out your local gyms because they'll be reducing the cost of their summer memberships this month.

It's time to get out and explore the local bargains as you celebrate the coming of warmer weather. Save on these food and non-food items to get your summer party started.

Deals of the Month: July

Aaahhh! It's time for those summer barbecues. Can't you smell the charcoal already? What could be better than hamburgers and hot dogs with all the fixings – especially if you can get all those "fixings" on sale!

Check out the fabulous buys at your grocery stores in July.

- ☐ Chips
- ☐ Soda pop
- ☐ Bottled water
- ☐ Tea bags
- ☐ Ground beef
- ☐ Hot dogs
- ☐ Ketchup
- ☐ Mustard
- ☐ Barbecue sauce
- ☐ Hamburger and hot dog buns
- ☐ Popsicles and other frozen novelty treats
- ☐ Ice cream

Don't forget your fresh summer produce – also on sale in the produce aisles:

- ☐ Green beans
- ☐ Lettuce
- ☐ Cucumbers
- ☐ Tomatoes

These necessary non-food items to complete your picnics also have special pricing in July:

- ☐ Paper plates
- ☐ Disposable cups
- ☐ Plastic eating utensils
- ☐ Napkins
- ☐ Charcoal Lighter Fluid
- ☐ Charcoal

If you need to replace any furniture, July is the month you'll find it on sale. Take advantage of all these wonderful deals this summer.

The deals are sizzling when the weather's hot!

Deals of the Month: August

Think, "Hot fun in the summertime" when it comes to grocery shopping. Foods you love to eat in the hot weather can be bought cheaply. Make room in your cupboard and refrigerator for the following items:

- ☐ American cheese
- ☐ Breakfast bars
- ☐ Chips
- ☐ Cookies
- ☐ Drinks — bottled water, iced tea mix and bags, soda, and drink boxes
- ☐ Ice cream
- ☐ Jelly
- ☐ Lunch meat
- ☐ Peanut butter
- ☐ Snack cakes
- ☐ Yogurt

Since August is the hottest month throughout most of the United States, fresh fruits and vegetables are ripe and ready to pick. Select plenty of firm, fresh produce at your local stores this month. Watch for great deals on:

- Apricots
- Blueberries
- Corn
- Cucumbers
- Eggplant
- Green beans
- Lettuce
- Peaches
- Raspberries
- Strawberries
- Summer squash
- Tomatoes
- Watermelon

Plan for lots of outdoor activities and water fun, thanks to savings on these items:

- Bathing suits, summer clothes and shoes
- Outdoor furniture and toys
- Pool supplies

August is also an opportune time to purchase a new laptop, so if yours is three or more years old, check out the great buys at your

DEALS OF THE MONTH:
September

With summer winding down, it is the perfect time to shop for warm-weather items. Labor Days are an excellent opportunity to find deals and see deep discounts from stores reducing their summer-related inventory items. Look for the follow items:

- ☐ Summer clothing
- ☐ Large appliances
- ☐ Grills
- ☐ Pool related items
- ☐ Outdoor furniture
- ☐ School supplies
- ☐ Bicycles
- ☐ Bedding and mattresses
- ☐ Airfare

Deals of the Month: October

Top items to consider in October:

- ☐ Early Amazon Prime Day – allegedly happens in October
- ☐ New cars
- ☐ Summer grills
- ☐ Halloween items
- ☐ Camping gear
- ☐ Jeans and fall related clothing

DEALS OF THE MONTH: November

November is one of the biggest food-shopping months due to the fact that the holiday we all love—Thanksgiving—comes toward the end of the month.

Lucky for you, there's plenty of sale pricing at the grocery store in November. You're going to have the best feast ever, thanks to the deals you'll get on the following food items:

- ☐ Baking supplies
- ☐ Broth and soups
- ☐ Butter
- ☐ Cake mixes and frostings
- ☐ Candy, marked down from Halloween
- ☐ Cheese
- ☐ Cranberries
- ☐ Dinner rolls
- ☐ Frozen pies
- ☐ Marshmallows
- ☐ Nuts
- ☐ Oranges
- ☐ Pears
- ☐ Pie crusts and fillings
- ☐ Pumpkins
- ☐ Pre-made dough
- ☐ Seasonings and spices
- ☐ Sweet potatoes
- ☐ Turkey

Some much-needed non-food items will also be on sale in November at your local grocery:

- Aluminum foil and plastic wrap
- Disposable baking pans

Bigger ticket items can be purchased at bargain basement pricing this month. Visit your home improvement store for deals on carpeting, flooring, tools, and plantings for your yard, especially bulbs and shrubs.

When you go to your discount store, you might want to check out prices for electronics and cookware because they'll be on special this month, too.

Happy November shopping!

Deals of the Month: December

The holidays are upon us! You'll do even more shopping this month than you did last. How will you stretch your dollars to make ends meet?

Don't worry, if you focus on what's on sale in December, you'll feed your family some great meals this holiday season.

With all those get-togethers and holiday baking, you're going to love the bargain pricing on these items:

- ☐ Baking supplies like baking chocolate, cooking oil, flour, nuts, sugar, and yeast
- ☐ Broccoli
- ☐ Butter
- ☐ Cake mixes and frostings
- ☐ Cauliflower
- ☐ Cheese
- ☐ Dried fruits
- ☐ Frozen Pies
- ☐ Grapefruits
- ☐ Ham
- ☐ Milk
- ☐ Mushrooms
- ☐ Oatmeal
- ☐ Oranges
- ☐ Papayas
- ☐ Pie crusts
- ☐ Pie filling
- ☐ Pomegranates

- ☐ Refrigerated cookie dough
- ☐ Soda
- ☐ Sweet potatoes

You might be surprised at the great deals you'll see on disposable baking pans, aluminium foil, and plastic wrap when you're doing your December grocery shopping.

It's likely you'll be doing at least some of your holiday gift shopping in December. If so, watch for some big mark-downs on computers, cookware, electronics, tools, toys, winter clothes, and winter coats.

Do you need a new vehicle? If so, December's the month to buy it. If you're the sportier type, good deals on motorcycles can also be had in December.

Enjoy these holiday savings this month! Happy holidays!